The Boys

GORDON GRAHAM

CURRENCY PRESS
SYDNEY

CURRENCY PLAYS

First published in 1994
by Currency Press Pty Ltd,
Gadigal Land, Suite 310, 46-56 Kippax Street, Surry Hills NSW 2010
Australia
enquiries@currency.com.au
www.currency.com.au
in association with
Griffin Theatre Company, Sydney.

Revised edition, 2012

Cataloguing-in-Publication data for this title is available from the National Library of Australia website: www.nla.gov.au.

Typeset by Dean Nottle for Currency Press.
Cover photograph by Michael Corridore.
Front cover shows Josh McConville.
Cover design by Katy Wall for Currency Press.
Currency Press acknowledges the Traditional Owners of the Country on which we live and work. We pay our respects to all Aboriginal and Torres Strait Islander Elders, past and present.

Contents

THE BOYS

Act One   1

Act Two   37

ACKNOWLEDGEMENTS

I wish to thank Sue Woolfe for her immeasurable help in the long and arduous editing process that this play's sensitive subject matter and complex structure demanded. My thanks go also to Alex Galeazzi, whose belief in the play helped rescue it from the oblivion to which it was consigned after the 1988 Playwrights' Conference, and whose untiring efforts led to its first production. Thanks go also to the dedicated group of actors who were involved in the various stages of the play's emergence, and to the late Tony Williams who, as my agent, was ceaseless in his enthusiasm for the work.

The Boys was first performed by the Griffin Theatre Company at the Stables Theatre, Sydney, on 28 February 1991 with the following cast:

SANDRA	Lynette Curran
GLENN	David Field
NOLA	Pamela Katt
MICHELLE	Lisbeth Kennelly
STEVIE	Peter Lehner
BRETT	David Wenham
JACKIE	Shani Wood

Director, Alex Galeazzi
Designer, Tim Kobin
Lighting Designer, Robert Connolly
Sound Design, John Gordon

CHARACTERS

BRETT SPRAGUE, late 20s
GLENN SPRAGUE, mid 20s
STEVIE SPRAGUE, early 20s
SANDRA SPRAGUE, late 40s, mother of Brett, Glenn and Stevie
MICHELLE, mid 20s
JACKIE, mid 20s
NOLA, about 18

SETTING

The backyard and living room of the Sprague home in an outer suburb.

The backyard is stark and arid, with barely a blade of grass. There is one withered tree, a Hills hoist, a stripped-down car body gradually merging into the ground, a couple of car seats, and a crude barbeque. The living room is a little warmer in atmosphere, full of mismatched furniture and bric-a-brac. Prominent in both settings is a battered cane lounge, which is moved between one location and the other.

The scenes in the living room take place over several months. Intercut with them are scenes in the backyard, which all take place on one day.

ACT ONE

SCENE ONE

Lights up on the living room. It is very early morning, Tuesday. MICHELLE *stands at the window, looking out anxiously.* SANDRA *is seated on the cane lounge with her feet up, and a blanket around her shoulders.*

MICHELLE: I have to know.

SANDRA: I understand how you feel, love, but it's not the first time the boys have stayed out.

MICHELLE: But the way they were carrying on yesterday. You couldn't help thinking. Something was bound to happen.

SANDRA: Just like always, eh? The men go off and do what they're going to do, and expect you to wait for them, as if that's all you've got to do.

MICHELLE: Been waiting long enough, haven't I?

> *There is a stirring at the back of the house.* SANDRA *gets up and goes to the doorway leading to the rear. She calls.*

SANDRA: Stevie! You get back to bed this minute! You've caused enough trouble already, and I'm not having you prowling around the house in that state. You get back to bed and sleep it off, whatever it is. [*She watches for a moment.*] Whatever it is. [*She moves back into the living room.*] What can he have been doing to himself? That mad look in his eye, and coming in through the bathroom window like that, as if he didn't know quite where he was. Almost like he was high on something.

MICHELLE: Maybe he is.

SANDRA: Out of his head, he is. Senseless.

MICHELLE: Do you think he needs a doctor?

SANDRA: Over my dead body. This is a family problem, and I'm not having any outsiders sticking their noses in.

MICHELLE: No, no, you're right. I'm just so anxious, that's all. About Brett. I mean the three of them have always done everything together, so, you know, whatever happened to Stevie…

From inside the house there comes another stirring sound. SANDRA
goes to the doorway. She reacts with alarm as NOLA *enters.* NOLA
*is wearing a nightie, and has a blanket around her shoulders. She
is visibly pregnant.*

SANDRA: Oh, Nola, love, what's wrong?

NOLA: [*sobbing*] It's not right. I didn't do anything to him.

SANDRA: Jesus, what's he done now?

NOLA: He kicked me. Nearly got the baby.

SANDRA: What's going on in his head?

NOLA: He stands there, looking down at me, and he says, 'You deserve it,
you bitch, you can count yourself lucky you're as useless as you are'.
Shit, what did he mean by that?

SANDRA: How could he call you a bitch?

NOLA: It was like I'd done something wrong.

MICHELLE: You were just in the line of fire.

NOLA: Was that scary. I mean with his clothes the way they were. All
ripped about and covered in muck. And all the raving he was doing,
hating everybody under the sun. Especially me.

> SANDRA *approaches the entrance to the rear of the house, and
> calls out.*

SANDRA: For God's sake Stevie, I could throttle you. [*She turns back
towards the others.*] Oh, what's the use? [*To* NOLA] You better get to
bed, love. You need your sleep more than any of us.

NOLA: No, don't want to. Not in there.

SANDRA: Yeah, you better have my bed. Wasn't going to go back to it
anyway.

MICHELLE: You sure, Sandra? The way you said you were feeling
yesterday?

SANDRA: No, I'll be alright. Much better now. Go on, Nola love.

NOLA: Thanks.

MICHELLE: Yeah, I'll come and tuck you in, okay?

> NOLA *and* MICHELLE *begin to move away.*

NOLA: Was there anything wrong in wanting someone that much? When
you've had to wait so long? When you've started to think that no-one
will ever turn up?

SANDRA: Yeah, I know, it's so hard on your own.

NOLA: You keep waiting and waiting, and you can't help thinking, well maybe he's the one. Maybe he'll do.

> NOLA *and* MICHELLE *leave.* SANDRA *lies back.*

SANDRA: Oh, these nights, that just go on and on, and nothing makes sense at all. [*Pause.*] I suppose you don't dare try make sense of it, because of the things you've seen, the things you suspect they're really capable of. You don't dare try and add it all up, specially not in the black of night. Same as you don't dare talk about it.

> *There is a loud knocking on the front door. Taken by surprise,* SANDRA *sits up and listens for a moment. The knocking is repeated.* JACKIE*'s voice is heard from outside.*

JACKIE: Will somebody open this door?

SANDRA: [*surprised*] Oh.

> SANDRA *gets up slowly and moves towards the door, now moving with some difficulty. The knocking is repeated louder.* SANDRA *opens the door, and* JACKIE *steps in abruptly. She is dressed in the uniform of a rent-a-car girl.*

JACKIE: Is Glenn here?

SANDRA: He's not with you?

> MICHELLE *enters, concerned.*

MICHELLE: Brett? [*She looks at* JACKIE, *disappointed.*] Oh, it's her.

JACKIE: [*to* MICHELLE] Have you seen him?

MICHELLE: Who?

JACKIE: [*angry*] Glenn, of course!

MICHELLE: Alright, I'm not a bloody mind-reader!

JACKIE: The idiot hasn't come home.

MICHELLE: Yeah, he probably couldn't take any more.

JACKIE: Is he here or not?

MICHELLE: No! Is that clear enough?

JACKIE: What about the others? Are they here?

MICHELLE: Why should you care about them now? You never have before.

JACKIE: Because they'll know where Glenn is!

SANDRA: I'm sure when Glenn feels like coming home to you he will. In the meantime I'm not going to go meddling in his life.

JACKIE *backs away, exasperated.*

JACKIE: I know something's been going on. I know what those three are like.

MICHELLE: Listen to Miss High and Mighty.

JACKIE: It makes me sick, what goes on around here.

MICHELLE: Well, stuff you. If you don't like it, go away.

JACKIE: Don't worry, I will.

MICHELLE: Great, see you around.

JACKIE: The only reason I came back to this place was because I thought I might give Glenn one last chance. Though after yesterday I can't imagine why.

MICHELLE: No?

JACKIE: They treated us like dirt yesterday. I don't know how the rest of you just go on taking it.

MICHELLE: Yeah, well, we all got our different ways of dealing with things. You're not as special as you think.

SANDRA: Yes, it's about time you learned that. You might get on with people better. You're dealing with a family here.

JACKIE: Don't worry, I'm going. This could be the last time you ever see me.

MICHELLE: Is that a promise?

JACKIE: And if Glenn does show up here, you can tell him, if that job I lined up means anything to him, he better turn up today and do some explaining.

MICHELLE: Hah, some job. Scrubbing out rent-a-cars.

JACKIE: It's a lot better than anything he ever had before! Yes, and what's more, you can tell him, this time he can go to the boss himself and do his own grovelling. See if Mr Sorenson wants to hear how tough it is coming from a family like this one.

SANDRA: The way you criticise us all the time, after everything we've done to make you feel welcome. I've always thought, one of these days you'll go too far.

JACKIE: I've gone too far? I put up with things no other decent girl would tolerate. Because I know he can't help where he comes from.

SANDRA: [*angry*] How dare you! Get out of here.

JACKIE: Yesterday, he slipped all the way back to the gutter.

SANDRA: Just go!

JACKIE: You think I want to stay around?

> JACKIE *leaves.*

SANDRA: Oh, that sharp tongue of hers, she can say some real hurtful things when she gets going. Doesn't seem to realise other people have feelings too.

MICHELLE: Yeah, poor Glenn, eh? Imagine copping that sort of stuff night after night.

> *The sound of a small car moving away outside.* MICHELLE *goes to the window and looks out.*

Bugger that Brett. Why does he always have to go and mess things up?

SANDRA: He's who he is, Michelle. And you can either love what's there, or…

MICHELLE: Don't get me wrong, I don't want anyone else. But jeez, it's hard knowing how to take it all.

SANDRA: No-one's saying it's easy. But sometimes you've just got to go on holding onto things, even when they do something that makes no sense at all. Go on gritting your teeth and taking it.

MICHELLE: Yeah, well, nobody can say I haven't given it my best shot, can they?

SANDRA: No, that's true, nobody can.

MICHELLE: But what good's it done? When the two of us finally got to be together again yesterday, what was there?

SANDRA: You feel awful, don't you? When they've gone and let you expect so much.

> *Pause.*

MICHELLE: You know, all the time I was visiting him while he was inside, everything seemed so full of hope. We'd hold hands, and somehow, he'd be telling me everything. Without saying a word. Was just the way his hand is, rough here, and smooth there, and the way he'd squeeze, confiding, somehow his hand was saying, 'Look, I don't care how things might have been before, but right now, from now on, anything's possible'. And you'd have to believe him.

SANDRA: I know. How could you help but believe?

MICHELLE: Was the same before, you know, those few months we had together, before he went in. Okay, he might have been hard to deal with a lot of the time, he's a hard man, but at the same time, there was this other side, he'd just let you glimpse sometimes. Was like looking into a window. Into something really gentle. And that's not something he'd let anybody see. Except me. He trusted me. I know that.

SANDRA: I believe you, love. That feeling when you know they've let you in on things. When they let you believe that just maybe there's a bit more to them than meets the eye. Yeah.

MICHELLE: But yesterday. Don't know where it all went. God knows what was going on with him. Was nothing gentle there.

SANDRA: No.

MICHELLE: When we finally got together in bed, after all that, it was like he was trying to push me into shape, make me into something else. And then at the end, after he'd got himself all worked up. Well, he couldn't do it. Was like there was nothing in him.

SANDRA: You know, you can't help thinking, maybe when a bloke first gets out, and he's all screwed up about sex, you'd be better keeping right out of his hair, just packing him straight off to Kings Cross to get it over with, with some girl he doesn't know. Better for all concerned.

MICHELLE: Except maybe the girl.

SANDRA: All that business in bed, well what's that matter really, when it comes right down to it? That's just the icing on the cake.

> *The sound of cars approaching rapidly, and pulling up suddenly outside. The slamming of car doors, rapid heavy footsteps, then heavy knocking on the front door, repeated.*

Well, I wonder who that is?

> MICHELLE *gets up and peeks through the venetian blinds.*

MICHELLE: Shit, it's the cops.

> *The knocking is repeated more heavily.*

SANDRA: Oh no. He's only been out of gaol a day.

> *Blackout.*

SCENE TWO

The previous afternoon. The backyard. STEVIE *struggles in, carrying the battered cane lounge. He is wearing ripped jeans and a heavy metal t-shirt. He places the lounge under the tree.* SANDRA *enters after him, walking slowly, as if in a weakened state.*

STEVIE: There ya are, Mum.

SANDRA: Thanks, Stevie. You're a good boy. [*Sinking down onto the cane lounge.*] Got to rest the poor old bag of bones. Reckon one of these days you'll have to put wheels on this thing and drag me round on it. Won't be able to get up at all.

STEVIE: Ah, no, Mum, you'll be right, the quack reckons. [*Pause. He paces around impatiently, as if waiting for somebody to arrive.*] Jeez, where are they?

SANDRA: Calm down, love. They probably stopped off at an early opener for their own celebration. Reckon poor Brett would have had his tongue hanging out for a couple of cold schooners after all that time.

STEVIE: Yeah, I reckon. Could do with one meself. Fuckin' Glenn, why couldn't he have picked me up on his way? Instead of that I'm stuck here, having to put up with her.

He gestures towards the house.

SANDRA: No, Nola's nice, love. You're very lucky to have her. You've got your own little family coming on.

STEVIE: Yeah, but there's all that chuckin' up in the mornings now, in my bedroom! I have to go runnin' off for basins and that. Just watchin' it I get sicker than she does.

SANDRA: You just have a think what it means, son, what's going on inside her. There's a new life swimming around in there, and you're its dad.

STEVIE: Yeah, you don't have to tell me.

SANDRA: So you just try and be nice to her. I know you've got it in you.

STEVIE: But whenever I want to watch somethin' on TV, she always turns on some other crap, and you won't let me change channels on her. Jeez, the stuff she goes for.

SANDRA: She needs to relax right now, love, it's that time of pregnancy.

STEVIE: Yeah, what about me, but? How come she always does it when there's somethin' good on? Hardly ever get to see 'The Footy Show' now.

> NOLA *enters.*

NOLA: Stevie.

STEVIE: Aw, what do you want now?

NOLA: I don't know, I just want to, you know, talk.

STEVIE: Yeah, well I was in before, talkin' to you and that. Did me best.

NOLA: Yeah, but then you came out here. In the middle of what we were saying.

> NOLA *sits down on a car seat.*

STEVIE: It's not fair, I reckon. Nothin' is.

NOLA: I just want to, like, be with you, that's all.

STEVIE: Yah, you don't ask much, do you?

SANDRA: Stevie, I told you. A pregnant woman needs the baby's daddy around looking after them both. It's like a deep hormonal need.

STEVIE: Yeah, but why me?

> MICHELLE *enters from the house. She is dressed up, and her hair has obviously been given a lot of attention, done in a slightly aggressive style.*

MICHELLE: Took so long getting me hair done, I was worried I was going to miss him. Took 'em hours to get this right. What do you think, eh?

SANDRA: Yeah, really nice, isn't it?

STEVIE: Hey, can I have a feel?

MICHELLE: No, keep your mouldy hands off it.

> STEVIE *touches* MICHELLE'*s hair. She pulls back.*

STEVIE: Aw, it feels like, yurk, slimy worms or somethin'.

MICHELLE: Leave it alone. Don't want you messing it up. That cost eighty bucks.

STEVIE: Jesus, you could buy a couple of bottles of Southern Comfort for that.

> *The sound of a small car approaching, and pulling up very close by.* STEVIE *jumps up excitedly.*

They're here! They're here!

BRETT *and* GLENN *enter from the driveway.* BRETT *is dressed very much like* STEVIE, *and carries a cheap overnight bag.* GLENN *is dressed a little more neatly, and carries a carton of beer cans.*

Jesus, Brett, you're back, eh?

MICHELLE *rushes forward and hugs* BRETT. *He responds, and they embrace passionately.*

MICHELLE: Aw, Brett, it's all over, eh?

BRETT: Yeah. It's been a hard bastard.

MICHELLE *and* BRETT *continue their embrace.* STEVIE *shuffles close by, trying to attract* BRETT's *attention.*

STEVIE: Yeah, Brett, welcome home, eh? Fuckin' beauty.

MICHELLE: Jesus, no more waiting, eh?

BRETT: No. No more waiting. You wouldn't believe how much I missed you. [*He pulls back and stares at* MICHELLE *for a moment.*] What happened to your hair?

MICHELLE: You like it?

BRETT: Looks like a dingo's breakfast.

MICHELLE: Aw, gee, thanks.

BRETT *goes over to* SANDRA.

BRETT: And how are you, Mum? Jeez it's good to see you again, you old duck.

BRETT *bends down to give* SANDRA *a hug and a kiss.* STEVIE *moves in quickly, trying to join the conversation, but is ignored.*

STEVIE: Yeah, Brett, and it's good to see you, mate.

SANDRA: Sorry I didn't get in to see you much, but after those first few visits, well, that bus ride started taking so much out of me, I can't tell you.

BRETT: Yeah, those fuckin' buses, they make you feel like you're in prison livin' out here.

SANDRA: And then, with all the hospital lately, and having to rest a lot. Well, it just wasn't in me.

BRETT: Eh? Just how bad are you?

SANDRA: Oh, I'm alright, don't you worry. Probably just got a bit run-down, they reckon.

BRETT: Jesus, nobody ever tells me nothin', do they?

GLENN: Yeah, well, we didn't want to worry you, mate.

BRETT: Bugger it, I got a right to know.

SANDRA: Come on, Brett, there's no need to worry about anything now. This is supposed to be a happy day, a celebration, like.

BRETT: Yeah, alright, alright. I just got a lot to sort out.

> *He rips open the beer carton and takes out a can. He opens it and takes a drink.* GLENN *moves in and takes a can for himself.*

Like no-one telling me you're sick. And fuckin' Glenn lettin' it slip he's not living here no more. Goes out of his way to break up the family, just when it ought to be stayin' together.

GLENN: Hey, come on, you can't have a go at me for leaving. I got me own life to lead too, you know.

BRETT: Goes off to live in his town house. Shit. It's in the middle of a fuckin' paddock and they call it a town house!

> *He laughs.*

SANDRA: Come on, Brett, that's enough.

BRETT: I'm just sayin' what's on me mind. After a year in that hole, I reckon I'm allowed.

SANDRA: Just don't go too far.

BRETT: And the fuckin' ultimate insult. Jesus! After all the fuckin' man-hours we put into doin' up his Premier he lets his bitch twist his arm into trading it in on a little Jap shit-box. A Corolla! And then he comes to pick me up in it.

GLENN: Hey, just watch what you're sayin' about me chick, alright?

BRETT: Christ. Can you imagine how I felt, sittin' in a car like that?

GLENN: I mean you're talkin' about Jackie, not just any moll.

BRETT: A Corolla! What if some bastard had seen me?

> STEVIE *approaches the beer carton.*

STEVIE: Hey, I reckon I might have one of them too.

> BRETT *places a hand over the opened end of the carton.*

BRETT: Eh? Why should I give you a beer, you little bastard?

STEVIE: What have I done wrong?

BRETT: Me wheels, mate. Me weapon. You let them bastards race off with it, just like that.

STEVIE: But there was proper legal papers, and there was four of 'em.

BRETT: Well, you should have paid me instalments like I asked.

STEVIE: Aw yeah, what with, me dole?

SANDRA: Now come on, Brett, be fair. You owed so much on it there wasn't much Stevie could do.

> BRETT *finally throws a beer to* STEVIE *who, taken by surprise, fumbles it and drops the catch.*

BRETT: It's the principle of the thing. The principle. That was the meanest, ugliest fuckin' V8 ute in the whole fuckin' state, and you let 'em take it away. Was the only thing I was livin' for in that stinkin' hole.

MICHELLE: That wasn't what you told me.

BRETT: Eh? Well, yeah, and you.

> MICHELLE *moves in closer and puts her arm around* BRETT*'s shoulder.*

MICHELLE: What's important now is just getting on with things.

BRETT: Without a car? Jesus, everythin's fallin' apart around here.

GLENN: Mate, it's not that bad. Come on, sink a few of these, eh, and we'll have a bit of a barbie.

> BRETT *paces around the backyard, as if trying to re-establish his territory. He notices* NOLA.

BRETT: Hey, who's this?

STEVIE: Oh, her, that's just, um, that's Nola.

BRETT: Well, you been busy, haven't you, you dirty little bastard.

STEVIE: Aw, don't you start.

SANDRA: Your brother's found himself a nice girlfriend at last, Brett. Starting a family all of his own, he is.

STEVIE: She's not me girlfriend, she isn't, not really.

NOLA: Aw, Stevie, that's not fair.

STEVIE: I'm just sayin' how it is. We're splittin' up. Matter of fact we have sort of split up already.

NOLA: We have not split up!

STEVIE: I say we've split up. I've got some rights too, you know, whatever anybody else might think.

> NOLA *gets up and begins moving away. She is near tears.*

NOLA: Aw, why do you have to go and say things like that in public, Stevie? What about the way I feel, eh?

SANDRA: Stevie, if you're really splitting up, then you can leave, because Nola's staying here to have your baby.

NOLA *moves away, beginning to cry.*

STEVIE: Aw, no, now she's bawlin' again. Shit.

NOLA *leaves.* MICHELLE *goes to follow her.*

MICHELLE: I'll look after her.

STEVIE: Yeah, somebody better.

MICHELLE *leaves.*

SANDRA: Stevie! Get in there and look after your girlfriend.

STEVIE: Aw!

STEVIE *slinks away into the house.*

SANDRA: If there's one thing in my life I'm proud of it's the way I've drummed it into you boys, you don't mistreat women!

BRETT: [*to* GLENN] Jesus, where did he find her?

SANDRA: And I'm not seeing it all go down the drain now. I'm bloody not! The same rules still go around here.

GLENN: Was when he was still driving your car around. He went down to watch 'em do wheelies one night! You know, down the big intersection where they put oil on the road.

BRETT: [*laughing*] Aw, yeah, used to love that, I was king of that place, they used to call me The Terminator.

GLENN: [*laughing disparagingly*] Hah, you reckon?

SANDRA: So I don't want to hear mean things said about that little girl. And that goes for you two, just as much as him.

GLENN: [*completely ignoring* SANDRA] Anyway, some bugger had given her the elbow, and she was cryin' her eyes out, and Stevie reckons she just crawled into the car with him, uninvited. [*He laughs.*] And they've been together ever since, and there's nothing he can do to get rid of her. Especially not now.

BRETT *laughs, contemptuously.*

BRETT: Yeah, that'd be right. Our Stevie. I can see it's really made a man of him.

SANDRA: You're down on everybody, aren't you? Well, let me tell you, Brett, Stevie's done real good. And he's had to be head of the family with you two gone.

BRETT: Hah, it's a wonder any of youse are still alive.

SANDRA: No, no, he's been a real surprise packet.

BRETT: Well then, looks like I needn't have bothered comin' back. Looks like nobody's missed me.

SANDRA: No, no, you've been missed. No doubt about that. But I'm just saying, you ought to show everyone a bit more love.

BRETT: Yeah, yeah.

SANDRA: Including Michelle.

BRETT: Where's she got to, then? I'm supposed to sit out here waitin', am I, after a whole year? Jesus, I'm ready for some action.

SANDRA: She'll be back out as soon as she settles Nola down. She's a real responsible girl, that one.

BRETT: Reckon I might just go and give her a hurry-up. Remind her what she's here for, eh?

    BRETT *leaves.*

GLENN: You goin' alright, Mum?

SANDRA: I should be happy as Larry, shouldn't I? But he gets so wound up sometimes, and if things aren't how he wants 'em to be…

GLENN: No, I'll try and keep him in line a bit.

SANDRA: That's real good of you, son. To do that with so much else on your plate.

GLENN: Well, he is me brother.

SANDRA: And how are you and Jackie, anyway? Still getting on alright?

GLENN: Yeah, yeah, alright, I mean nothing's perfect, you know, but all things considered, yeah, not too bad.

SANDRA: They're a lot of hard work, aren't they, relationships? But you can only do your best.

GLENN: I'll have to duck off and pick her up in a little while. She's putting a few things together for the barbecue. Salads and that. Really making an effort.

SANDRA: Ah, you got a good one there, love. A real good one, there, deep down, you stick with her.

    BRETT *re-enters, rapidly and angrily.*

BRETT: Women! Shit!

GLENN: What happened, mate?

BRETT: Jesus, what's wrong with her priorities? I go in there really dyin' for it after all that time, and she's stuffin' round makin' a cup of tea for that stupid dag of Stevie's.

GLENN: Well, you wouldn't have had to wait all that long, would you, while she finished? A cup of tea?

BRETT: It's the principle of the thing. I told her what I wanted to do and she wouldn't.

SANDRA: So now you've had a fight with her, ten minutes after getting back together. You got to learn to hang onto that temper of yours.

BRETT: I just can't stand all that fussin' around over each other chicks do sometimes. It's almost like they're bein' each other's mums.

SANDRA: Well, I'm ashamed of you, I really am. Michelle practically worships the ground you walk on, and just because she happens to be showing a bit of compassion for someone in trouble, you do your block. There's a few more things in life than just your natural urges, son. Isn't that so, Glenn?

GLENN: Aw, yeah, for sure.

BRETT: Yah, what would you know?

SANDRA: Now you get in there and apologise to her.

BRETT: Me?

SANDRA: I wanted this to be a happy day. I wanted to enjoy having my family around me again, so I could see the struggle's all been worth it. Are you going to let me down?

> BRETT *moves away, towards the house.*

BRETT: Alright, alright!

> BRETT *leaves.*

GLENN: Jesus. Already.

SANDRA: Michelle will find a way to calm him down.

GLENN: Hope so.

SANDRA: Brett's a bit like your dad. Real firebrand, hair-trigger temper. But underneath there's a heart of gold, and that's what a woman's got to concentrate on, if she wants to get anywhere with a man like that.

GLENN: Don't reckon Dad's heart turned out to be gold.

SANDRA: Well, it took a while to see that.

    BRETT *enters, even angrier than before.*

BRETT: Would you believe it? Now she's pissed off.

SANDRA: She's probably just gone to the bathroom, love. To compose
    herself.

BRETT: I've just been right through the house. She's not there, okay?

GLENN: Well, calm down, mate. She's got to be somewhere.

BRETT: Yeah, and I reckon I know where, too. Back to that scumface
    with the tow truck.

GLENN: No, mate, no way.

BRETT: She was on with him all the time I was inside, wasn't she, and
    you bastards didn't tell me.

GLENN: No, you're wrong. As usual.

SANDRA: Yes, Brett, she's been absolutely faithful.

BRETT: Pig's arse! Chicks wouldn't know the meaning of the word. Jesus,
    if she thinks she can get away with that. Okay, give me the keys to
    that shit-heap Corolla, will you, I'm going to go over and sort her out.

GLENN: No, sorry, you can't have 'em. I've got to go and pick up Jackie.

BRETT: Let the bitch wait. Since when do you let a chick tell you when
    you can come and go?

GLENN: I want to pick her up! That's just the way it is. Look, you don't
    need the car anyway, she won't have gone far on foot. Run after her.

BRETT: Eh? Me, on foot? Me? I'm not goin' to lower meself, runnin' round
    the street like some deadshit jogger. Come on, I need the fuckin' car!

GLENN: No!

BRETT: That bitch of yours has got you by the balls. Pathetic!

GLENN: Hey, just cut it out, will you? Knock off all that stuff about Jackie.

BRETT: All I want's the car, mate, I don't give a shit about your stupid
    moll.

SANDRA: Brett! That's enough! You don't go talking about your brother's
    girlfriend like that.

BRETT: Aw, what am I supposed to do, but, Mum? She's over there with
    that animal, and I'm stuck here without wheels. Come on, Glenn, be
    reasonable. Look, okay, we'll both go. We'll go and find Michelle,
    and then we'll pick up Jackie.

GLENN: Jackie's waiting. Get the bus.

BRETT: Aw yeah, scared of a fight, eh? And scared big bad Jackie'll tell you off. What are ya, anyway, gutless?

SANDRA: Brett. Will you just get a hold of yourself? Have a bit of sense. Remember the last time you had a blue with someone? You go round there punching heads, you'll go back inside for another year. And won't that be fun for us all?

BRETT: Aw, jeez, Mum, I just want to stand up for me rights. It's only natural.

SANDRA: And she's not round there anyway, you dill, she's been living here the whole time, living for nothing else but the day you got out. I've really got to know her while you've been inside.

BRETT: Yeah?

SANDRA: Yeah. And she's probably gone for a walk to clear her head, that's the sort of thing she does when she's got troubles. Maybe that's the sort of thing you should do when you get like this!

BRETT: Walk?

GLENN: You're goin' to have to accept it, mate. You can't push me round no more. Your little brother's grown up while you been away.

> GLENN *takes out the car keys.*

BRETT: Aw yeah? You still need your mum to fight your battles for you.

> GLENN *moves further away.*

GLENN: I mean it's great to have you back. I mean that. But I'll tell you. One thing I didn't miss was you throwin' your weight around all the time so you always got your own way. Well, you're not the big boss anymore, mate.

> *He moves closer to the gate.*

BRETT: Say hullo to Jackie for me. If you're brave enough you can ask her why she never come to visit me in gaol.

GLENN: Ask her yourself.

> GLENN *leaves.*

BRETT: Aw, yeah, thinks he's real big-time now, doesn't he? He's only me little brother. Christ, is he in for a takin' down.

SANDRA: Brett love, come on. Get yourself another drink. Get one for your mum as well and come and sit down here. [*She makes room for him on the lounge.*] We'll have a good old yarn about this and that. Just like we used to.

BRETT: Yeah, alright.

BRETT *takes two cans from the carton and hands one to* SANDRA.

SANDRA: Thanks, love.

BRETT *sits down on the end of the lounge. They open the cans and begin drinking.*

Here's to you, son. [*Raising her can*] Welcome home.

BRETT: Thanks, Mum.

They take a couple of sips and BRETT *relaxes a little.*

SANDRA: In a bit of a state, aren't you?

BRETT: Yeah.

SANDRA: Had a rough time inside?

BRETT: Yeah. [*Pause.*] Yeah, did a bit. Aw, some of those blokes in there. Crazy, they are. Do anythin' to anybody, doesn't matter how tough you are.

SANDRA: Being tough isn't the point.

BRETT: You got no idea. I'm talkin' about boilin' fat chucked in some-body's face, and ground glass in their food, and blokes bein' given ODs deliberate like, and, shit... I don't think I want to tell you any more.

SANDRA: All some people can do is hurt other people.

BRETT: Makes you have a real hard look at yourself.

SANDRA: That's something, anyway.

BRETT: You find yourself thinkin', why the fuck am I here? You think, all the shit I gone through in me life, and look where it's got me. [*He takes another drink.*] Like, I lost a whole year out of me life 'cause some dickhead dented me car.

SANDRA: You lost a whole year out of your life because of what you did to the dickhead.

BRETT: 'Cause of a little thing like that dent I lost me freedom. A year out of me life.

SANDRA: So you regret it. You won't do it again?

BRETT: Nah.

SANDRA: We got an agreement on that? You promise?

BRETT: Yeah, 'course I do.

SANDRA: Well. Maybe you really have come to your senses.

BRETT: [*laughing*] Yeah, too right I have. Next time I do me block and wipe some bastard out it's goin' to be over something big, like a payroll.

SANDRA: [*alarmed*] Brett! Don't you talk rubbish. I don't want to hear you even joking about that sort of criminal stuff.

BRETT: [*laughing*] No, no, Mum, just jokin', it's alright.

SANDRA: Well, don't joke like that. I'm not up to it, after what you put me through already.

BRETT: Yeah, alright, sorry, just havin' a lend of you. Don't worry, I'm no crim, whatever anybody says.

SANDRA: Nobody says you're a crim.

BRETT: Don't they? Reckon after a year in the boob, that's just what they will be sayin'. Behind me back, anyway.

SANDRA: Don't, love. Don't get caught up in being all bitter. Put it behind you, you got so much going for you, still.

BRETT: Hah, me?

SANDRA: Yeah. You got your health. A good brain, when you can be bothered using it. A bit of get-up-and-go. And Michelle with you.

BRETT: You reckon?

SANDRA: Yeah, Brett, I do reckon. The way she talked about nothing else but you, she just about bored us rigid.

>   BRETT *takes a long drink*

BRETT: Alright. Alright. But you can't help worryin'. Specially when you're inside. Knowin' what she might be capable of. Jesus, she'd still be in the gutter if it wasn't for me, you realise that?

SANDRA: Well, people who live in glass houses shouldn't throw stones.

BRETT: I'm not talkin' about chuckin' no rocks at no-one. I'm just sayin'. I expect me chick to behave herself when I'm off the scene. Is that too much too ask?

>   *Blackout.*

SCENE THREE

The living room, early the following evening. NOLA *is lying on the cane lounge.* SANDRA *enters carrying two cups of tea. She hands one to* NOLA.

SANDRA: There you are, love.

NOLA: Thanks. You sure you ought to be doing so much, the way you was so wobbly on your feet before?

SANDRA: It's alright, I got me second wind. [*She takes a sip of tea.*] I can imagine them, all those people. Baying like dogs, they'll be. Howling for blood. But they're wrong. Those boys never done that. Only a maniac would do something like that, and my sons aren't maniacs.

NOLA: No.

SANDRA: The cops were just looking for something to stick on them, just because the boys like to let off a bit of steam now and again. They found that poor girl this morning, and they said to themselves, those Sprague boys, let's get 'em.

> *Pause. They sip their tea.*

NOLA: You make a great cup of tea, Sandra.

SANDRA: Aw, thanks, love, thanks for saying so. You make it double strength, you see, and then you top it up with hot water at the end. That's the secret.

NOLA: Who'd have thought of that, eh, without bein' told?

SANDRA: Well, that's just one of those things you know. Sort of in your blood.

NOLA: You reckon it would work with a tea bag?

SANDRA: No, no, don't like tea bags. With tea bags, you can't make it like you want. You've just got to cop whatever comes out.

NOLA: Yeah.

> *Pause. They sip their tea.*

SANDRA: [*suddenly angry*] It's just not true! I don't care what they say. Those boys wouldn't have done that to a woman.

NOLA: No, they wouldn't. 'Course they wouldn't.

SANDRA: What happened to her, that's something else again. Only somebody mad could do that. There are that sort of men, too, I know, and a girl's got to be on the lookout with 'em, and know when to say stop.

NOLA: If she has any say in it.

> JACKIE *enters. She stands looking around, then flops down onto a chair. The others watch.*

SANDRA: What's happened? Have you seen Glenn?

JACKIE: They arrested him.

SANDRA: Oh, no.

JACKIE: I thought you would have heard.

NOLA: Nah, people like us don't get told nothing.

JACKIE: You ought to count yourselves lucky they've left you alone. It's been so humiliating.

SANDRA: What?

JACKIE: In public! There I was this morning, at the counter, fixing up this really nice man with a Commodore Executive. Really well-dressed he was, silk tie and everything, well spoken. And in the middle of it all, in walk three policemen! Can you imagine, right into your place of work!

SANDRA: Yeah, well, they barged in here early this morning too, you know.

JACKIE: But this was with decent, respectable people looking on, don't you understand? People seeing me being questioned like I was associated with something criminal. 'Well,' I said to them, really firm I was, 'would you mind coming out the back, please?' And they did, too, they could tell from that they weren't just dealing with some grubby little moll they could push around.

NOLA: Really showed them, did you?

JACKIE: But oh, what I went through in those few moments. What I suffered. After all I've worked for.

SANDRA: We got other things on our minds right now. Like the boys, you know?

JACKIE: Alright, I'm worried about them too. Do you think I haven't got any feelings? I had to stand there this afternoon and watch them drag Glenn away. I had to watch him cry.

NOLA: Really messed up your day, didn't he?

JACKIE: The idiot, he came back to our flat, just after I came home from work. The police must have been watching. They pounced on him.

SANDRA: Was Brett with him?

JACKIE: No. At least Glenn had the sense not to make things worse by hanging around with the others.

SANDRA: I'm surprised. Those boys have always hung around together.

JACKIE: Yes, and that's what everybody's going to think, too, isn't it? How's poor Glenn ever going to convince anyone he's innocent when he's got people saying, 'Well, those Sprague brothers, they've always done everything together'.

SANDRA: But they're all innocent. You know that, don't you?

JACKIE: I know how easily led Glenn is.

SANDRA: Well, you really believe in standing by him, don't you? Any man with you for a friend wouldn't need enemies.

JACKIE: I just want to know the truth. Doesn't that matter?

SANDRA: The truth's staring you in the face, love. The rest of us already know it.

JACKIE: Do you? I don't know how. I mean I've lived with Glenn a while now. I've seen all his highs and lows, held onto him at four o'clock in the morning. But know him? Know what really makes him tick? Know how he looks at a pretty girl when I'm not there, or what he'd say about her to his brothers? Maybe you just see what you'd like to see.

SANDRA: But you know things are true because you can feel it, everywhere, like in the pit of your stomach and the tips of your fingers, and the soles of your feet. That's how you know what's true.

JACKIE: You don't know.

SANDRA: [*emphatic*] I know my sons are innocent!

> JACKIE *opens her handbag and takes out a packet of cigarettes. She takes out a cigarette and lights it, then has a long puff.*

JACKIE: Look, see, I'm smoking again, because of all this. I hadn't touched one for six months.

> MICHELLE *enters hurriedly.*

MICHELLE: What's happening?

SANDRA: Oh, they've got Glenn too, now, love. They grabbed him at the town house.

MICHELLE: When?

SANDRA: [*to* JACKIE] Wasn't that long ago, was it?

JACKIE: Five past five. I remember looking at the kitchen clock.

MICHELLE: [*surprised*] You were there?

JACKIE: Yes.

MICHELLE: How come you're here now? You must have made them like you.

JACKIE: They'd already spoken to me at the office. They knew I wasn't going to do anything to obstruct.

MICHELLE: You weren't? What's wrong with you?

JACKIE: They'd come to the flat to take Glenn away, and that's exactly what they were going to do, whatever anyone did. What was I supposed to do, pull the carving knife on them?

MICHELLE: Well yeah, I would have. Any normal person would have. Hell, I've just had six hours down at the cop shop, bein' stood over by the meanest bunch of fat, sweaty pigs you've ever seen in your life. Being called every dirty name in the book, slut, whore, bitch, slag, scum, being run up against the wall and having their hands feeling all over me. Threatened with twenty years for aiding and abetting a murderer. Shown pictures of that poor girl some animal did over. [*She breaks down.*] Aw, shit, you never seen anything like it, what they done to her, they just ripped her apart. [*She sobs, then collects herself.*] Being told that was what my boyfriend did. [*She accuses* JACKIE, *angrily.*] But they got nothing out of me! Nothing! And they won't, neither, because I believe in Brett, and I don't believe he's capable of doing something like that. And shit, if you believe Glenn could have, well, Jesus, what were you with him for in the first place?

JACKIE: I'm not saying I believe Glenn did it. Of course I'm not.

> MICHELLE *goes to a window, and pulls the curtains apart slightly. She points.*

MICHELLE: Look, see that white car right down near the corner? That's the police. The bastards drove me here, and now they're sitting there watching. All of us. They're sitting there thinking, 'You scum of the earth'!

JACKIE: But I'm not. We're not.

MICHELLE: Yeah, so why do you have to give in to them? Knuckle under?

SANDRA: I suppose we all have to cope with something like this in our own ways. Do what our hearts tell us. Just like the boys must be. Imagine how they feel, eh? Being thought capable of something like that.

MICHELLE: Yeah. Yeah. Kills you, doesn't it, thinking about that.

SANDRA: Yes. Yes it does. My sons being thought of like that. Any idea what's happened to Brett, love? Any idea at all?

> *Pause.*

MICHELLE: Yes, he's gone on the run. Gone bush.

SANDRA: [*excited*] Have you spoken to him?

MICHELLE: Yeah. This morning, when I left here. Took the shortcut down the back lane, and there he was. Came out from behind the bushes. Jeez, he looked rough. Was like he knew he was in for it, and he'd come back to say goodbye. He just said what he had to say, and told me to piss off, and he was gone again in thirty seconds.

SANDRA: And did he, well, mention me at all, or give you any message or anything?

> MICHELLE *considers for a moment then remembers, a little too suddenly.*

MICHELLE: Oh, yeah, for sure. Right, Sandra, yeah, he, er, sends his love, and, erm, he wants you to know he'll be thinking of you, wherever he is. Was really keen for me to pass that on, too.

SANDRA: Well, that's nice, anyway. Even at a time like this. He's a good boy at heart, whatever anybody says.

MICHELLE: Yeah. Nobody can say different, can they? So then off he goes at full gallop. Bounding over fences and running in front of trucks, aw, he was like a commando or something, a man with a mission. Out to save his skin.

SANDRA: Yeah, he could have been a war hero, you know, that boy, if he'd been born in a different time. Do you know where he was off to?

MICHELLE: Yeah, I got a rough idea, but I'm not saying now. Not with Miss Judas around. The cops spent all day trying to get it out of me and I'm not going to just drop it in her lap.

> JACKIE *stands up angrily.*

JACKIE: Don't you say that about me! I wouldn't. I might not like what's going on, but I wouldn't do that.

MICHELLE: No?

SANDRA: I'm sure Jackie's suffering just like the rest of us, Michelle. She just has a different way of showing it.

MICHELLE: Yeah, very different.

JACKIE: You don't know anything. You just don't know anything. You know what I did today for Glenn? Instead of going hysterical, I at least did something positive. Found out about what's going to happen. Charges and committal hearings and that sort of thing. Found out about legal aid, and what sort of plea to make.

SANDRA: Well, that was clever of you, anyway. Good on you.

JACKIE: I've got a few contacts, and I'm not afraid to use them.

MICHELLE: Wait a minute, what do you mean, what sort of plea to make? What else would it be but not guilty? ⸝

JACKIE: Well, I can't say exactly, I mean there are a few different ways to go, the lawyer says, and... well, it's complicated.

MICHELLE: Don't worry, I can see what's going on in your mind. Have Glenn plead not guilty and dob the others in. Well, it won't work, sweetheart, because those boys are innocent, and they'll stick together. It'll take more than you to break them up.

JACKIE: [*exasperated*] I just want things to be done sensibly, that's all! Not make everything ten times worse by behaving like a bunch of, well...

MICHELLE: What, a bunch of hopeless dickheads from the slums? A bunch of animals?

> JACKIE *moves away abruptly.*

JACKIE: I'm going. You keep putting words in my mouth and I'm sick of it!

SANDRA: You don't want to go, love. Back to your lonely flat at a time like this. You'll be climbing the walls. We can put you up somewhere. Come on, stay here, it seems only right,

JACKIE: No, I don't want to stay here. Thank you. That's the last thing I want.

MICHELLE: Alright. Great.

> JACKIE *moves closer to the door.*

JACKIE: I know, you people think I don't feel anything. You think I don't care about anyone except myself. Well, I've done a lot for Glenn, more than most women could have. And now. I'm seeing everything I've done just disintegrate because of... well, because of what they've been allowed to get away with here. Think of what that feels like. You know, put yourself in my shoes for a bit before you start judging me.

> JACKIE *leaves.*

SANDRA: How dare she say things like that! What they've been allowed to get away with! What does she know? Every day of my life since the boys came along, there's been only one thing on my mind. Bringing them up loving and kind. But, Jesus, it's not all up to me, is it? I'm only one person.

MICHELLE: And you done well, Sandra. There's a lot of good in them. Would most other blokes be any better?

SANDRA: She thinks so.

MICHELLE: Well, bugger her, eh? Let her do whatever she wants to do. Won't make a bit of difference. In the end she might find she's cut her own throat by getting on her high horse like that. Might lose Glenn. Hah, that'd serve her right, wouldn't it? And lose her job, too.

SANDRA: No, don't think like that, love. This is a sad enough business already, and it doesn't help to go wishing more anguish on someone else, no matter what they're like.

MICHELLE: Yeah, but when life does this to you, you want to lash out, see someone else get it in the neck.

SANDRA: I know, but we'll only get through this by sticking together.

MICHELLE: I'm just all wound up, you know, after being with the cops all day. Aw, they really know how to get to a woman. Just sex, sex, sex, you know, about Brett and me, filthy stuff you'd think only a pervert would want to talk about. Was like everything about my life was theirs for the taking. I feel invaded, sort of, trampled on inside.

SANDRA: Yeah, men like that, those cops, they'd know how to get at a woman, just as much as the men who did that awful thing.

MICHELLE: The feeling it gives you. Makes me want to just crawl into some big black hole and pull a rock over it.

SANDRA: Go to bed. Get some rest.

MICHELLE: Yeah, I'm going to. Going to take a couple of Serepaxes. Shit, haven't done that for a while. Even when I was waiting around for Brett to get out, at least there was a hope then, something to hold onto in the dark.

SANDRA: They're innocent. That's something to hold onto.

MICHELLE: Yeah.

SANDRA: And innocent people go free.

MICHELLE: I'm trying to believe that. Trying like hell. But after what went on today… [*She moves away.*] See you in a while.

SANDRA: See you later.

MICHELLE *leaves. There is a pause.*

NOLA: Always happens, doesn't it? As soon as you get something that's even a bit okay. I mean I finally end up with Stevie. Who's alright, isn't he, really? He's not that bad to me most of the time, compared to, you know, how some blokes can be.

SANDRA: Yeah, Stevie's alright.

NOLA: But as soon as I start getting me life sorted out a bit, along comes this. It can't be just my bad luck, can it?

SANDRA: I don't know, Nola.

NOLA: I got a bloke, right. I'm nothing much, so it takes me a while, and I have to go through a lot of shit first. But I got Stevie, and he doesn't bash me up, and we might not do much, but at least there's someone there. And that's a lot better than no-one, isn't it?

SANDRA: I think so.

NOLA: And there's the baby, too. All that coming. And if it all turns out miserable, at least there'll be this little kid there. And who knows, my kid might even turn out to be alright, might even be nice to me. Hey, might even be someone who likes me.

SANDRA: That's the greatest love there is, between a mum and her children. It's the love that never dies.

> *Blackout.*

SCENE FOUR

The previous afternoon. The backyard. SANDRA *lies back on the cane lounge.* BRETT *sits on a car seat, drinking from a can. He looks up as* STEVIE *enters.*

BRETT: Any sign of her?

STEVIE: No, mate.

BRETT: Stupid bitch. Goes charging off just 'cause I laid down the law to her.

STEVIE: Yeah, doesn't it shit you when they do that?

BRETT: So I'm supposed to sit round on me arse, waitin' for her. I mean, does she want me or not?

STEVIE: Drive you round the bend, don't they? When you're really dyin' for it they piss off, and when you can't stand havin' 'em around they're all over you like a rash.

BRETT: Yeah. Jesus, you got your problems, I reckon, with that one of yours.

STEVIE: Can't stand much more of it, mate, I'm tellin' you.

BRETT: I'd piss her off like that. [*He snaps his fingers.*] You don't want to take shit from anybody.

STEVIE: Yeah, but on me own but. What am I supposed to do? With you and Glenn gone. You just have to walk down the street, not doin' nothin', and somebody'll start givin' you a hard time.

BRETT: Not me, they don't. Let's see 'em try.

> SANDRA *looks up.*

SANDRA: Stevie's had it real rough with you away, Brett. Had a rough time.

STEVIE: Yeah. Couldn't enjoy meself or nothin'. On me own. You know, you go into town like we used to. Hang round the shoppin' mall, check out the good-lookin' chicks. On your own, all you get's fuckin' laughed at, you know, gawked at like you was the lowest form of life. And it gives me the shits, it does, I'm sick of it.

BRETT: Yeah, it's a bitch, isn't it? Lots of people aren't worth nothin', the way they treat you.

SANDRA: I reckon the best thing you boys can do is go out and have a good time together, like in the old days.

STEVIE: [*excited*] Can we, Brett? Can we?

BRETT: Yeah, for sure. I'm rarin' to go. Don't know about Glenn, but. Reckon he's forgotten how.

SANDRA: Well, Glenn's doing things his own way now. These days there's other ways a man can run his life.

BRETT: That stupid stuck-up bitch. Got him by the balls, she has. [*He leans over confidentially to* STEVIE.] I'd like to know what goes on in their bed at night.

STEVIE: [*sniggering*] Haw, yeah.

BRETT: I reckon she probably gets on top!

SANDRA: Brett!

BRETT: Aw, shit, sorry Mum.

SANDRA: Anyway, what does it matter who's on top?

BRETT: But no, Glenn couldn't really have sunk that low, could he? Not me brother, no.

> MICHELLE *enters, tentatively.*

Well, shit, you come back. Was starting to think you must have gone off ridin' shotgun on your boyfriend's F100.

> MICHELLE *stops in her tracks.*

MICHELLE: That isn't fair, Brett. I dropped him when I met you. Haven't seen him since.

SANDRA: See, Brett?

MICHELLE: I went for a walk, that's all. Wanted to clear my head.

SANDRA: See?

BRETT: Walk? Around here?

MICHELLE: Better than staying around and having my head bitten off.

BRETT: But you come back anyway.

MICHELLE: Yeah, because I know you're not really like that.

BRETT: You reckon?

MICHELLE: And I wanted to be here for when you finally start to unwind.

BRETT: Unwind? I wanted to unwind, didn't I, I was dyin' for it, only you was stuffin' round makin' a cup of tea.

MICHELLE: Well, I'm here now, aren't I? So how about it, are you going to enjoy being back with us?

SANDRA: Good on you, love. You tell him.

BRETT: Alright, alright!

> MICHELLE *takes a beer from the carton and sits down next to* BRETT. *She puts an arm around him, then raises her beer can and clinks it against his.*

MICHELLE: So let's start off again, shall we? Welcome home. Welcome home, you big shit.

BRETT: Alright, here's lookin' up you, ya mad bitch. [*Raising his glass in response.*] Yeah, I reckon you was worth waitin' for.

> *They drink.*

MICHELLE: Suppose I must be mad, mustn't I? Don't know what I'm doing with you, sometimes.

BRETT: Don't ya? Don't ya? Jeez, you must have a bad memory then?

> BRETT *wraps his arm around* MICHELLE *and begins getting carried away very quickly, forcing her downwards in a passionate embrace. She slides out of his grip.*

MICHELLE: Hey, hang on, Brett, your mum's here, remember?

BRETT: So? I reckon the old dear knows a few things about the facts of life, isn't that right, Mum?

SANDRA: Come on, Stevie. Why don't we go inside and see how Nola is.

STEVIE: I know how she is!

SANDRA: Come on, those two have got things to talk about.

> BRETT *resumes his embrace of* MICHELLE, *even more passionate than before.* STEVIE *watches.*

STEVIE: Yeah, I can see that.

> SANDRA *and* STEVIE *leave.* BRETT *and* MICHELLE *continue their embrace for a little longer.*

MICHELLE: Mmm, that feels nice.

BRETT: Yeah.

> *They pull back a little.*

MICHELLE: Was never the same in that courtyard, with all those people around, and kids shouting so loud I could hardly hear what you were saying.

BRETT: Nah.

> MICHELLE *touches* BRETT'*s face.*

MICHELLE: Ah, the real thing, eh, after all that imagining.

BRETT: Yeah.

MICHELLE: Sometimes I'd come home after one of those visits, and ah, me mind would just be going round and round and round, full of all those plans we made. And I'd think of you, in your cell, and I'd get this little kind of buzz, 'cause I knew you'd probably be thinking about them too.

BRETT: Probably, yeah.

> MICHELLE *pulls back from* BRETT *again.*

MICHELLE: So what's going on, Brett? I mean it's happening, we're here, this is what we've waited for. And yet after all that, you come on really heavy with me, like you wanted to knock my head off, and then you do all this jealousy bit, when I haven't done anything to deserve it.

BRETT: Yeah?

MICHELLE: Yeah. And lots of other girls would have.

BRETT: You don't have to tell me that.

MICHELLE: I mean, a couple of months together wasn't long, was it? I hardly even got to know you properly before you went inside. But I wanted to know you.

BRETT: Trying to save me, are ya? Save me from meself.

MICHELLE: I kept thinking, if only we'd managed to get away up the coast that time, if only you hadn't got all caught up with that bloke over your stupid fender. We'd have been sleeping on beaches, and catching fish, and breathing the salty air, and just, going, wherever we wanted to. Might not ever have come back.

BRETT: 'Course we'd have come back. This is home.

MICHELLE: Well, maybe. But what I'm saying is, you'd have felt different. You'd have realised there's a bit more to things than just hanging round on street corners.

BRETT: [*laughing*] Hah, what, nature and all that stuff? You and your walks, eh, talkin' to the trees?

MICHELLE: You'll understand, one day.

BRETT: Where'd you walk to this time, eh, when you pissed off just before? Down to look at the dump, have a bit of a whiff? Down to the old drive-in? Hah, you could pretend all those little posts were trees, couldn't you, reckon that'd really turn you on.

MICHELLE: You have to know how to look.

BRETT: [*dismissive*] Yah.

MICHELLE: I found one little pool of water, I suppose you could call it a swamp, just across from where they're building the overpass. And there were a couple of trees sticking out of it, and it was perfectly still, and yet somehow it was shimmering.

BRETT: You're mad, you are, I said so before.

MICHELLE: And I stared at it for a while, and I thought, bloody Brett, if he could see this, he'd calm down too. So I came back.

BRETT: Good thing you did, too.

> *They resume their embrace with increasing passion, and soon slide down onto the grass.*

MICHELLE: Do you think maybe we should go inside? Your mum's kept your room just like you left it.

BRETT: Yeah, Christ yeah, awwgh!

> JACKIE *and* GLENN *enter.* JACKIE *is carrying a couple of tupperware containers.*

JACKIE: Well, there they are, the happy couple.

> BRETT *looks up, though stays entwined with* MICHELLE.

BRETT: How are you, stranger?

JACKIE: Great, Brett, just great. How's yourself?

BRETT: All pumped up ready for action. No bastard better stand in me way.

> BRETT *and* MICHELLE *resume their kissing.* JACKIE *turns away.*

JACKIE: I've made some salads. I think I'll put them in the fridge until the barbecue gets going.

> BRETT *looks up again from* MICHELLE.

BRETT: Yeah, you do that.

> JACKIE *moves closer to the house.*

Hey, I really missed you, you know that? All the time I was in the boob I was really lookin' forward to seein' your smilin' face. But maybe I was sick the day you come to visit, eh?

> JACKIE *turns back for a moment.*

JACKIE: I would have visited you, as a matter of fact. Only Glenn didn't want me to.

> JACKIE *leaves.*

BRETT: That true?

GLENN: It's complicated.

BRETT: I don't suppose it could be true, could it? You couldn't make her do nothin'.

GLENN: Yah, stuff ya!

> BRETT *laughs derisively.* GLENN *gets himself a can from the carton and opens it. He takes a drink.* STEVIE *enters.*

Look, just stop it, will you? Jackie's alright. Me and her got a few problems to sort out between us, and it doesn't help to have you stickin' your oar in. So just give us a go, eh?

BRETT: Aw, yeah? The two of youse are havin' a bust-up, are ya? What's it about, me bein' a bad influence and leadin' you astray?

GLENN: It's nothin' to do with you. You're not the centre of the world, whatever you might think.

BRETT: The sun shines out of me arsehole, mate.

GLENN: Look. Just go easy, that's all I'm askin'. I'm not sayin' there's problems, it's just, well, you know Jackie.

BRETT: Yeah, you're scared of her. Just like you're scared of me.

> BRETT *breaks free of* MICHELLE *and stands up.*

MICHELLE: Well, that was short and sweet.

BRETT: You'll keep. Right now I got business to attend to. You ready, mate? Let's go get a car.

GLENN: Eh?

BRETT: Feel dead without a set of wheels under me. Want to get somethin' big and mean, maybe somethin' all set up with mags and that. Big fuckin' rat 427 under the hood, four-barrel Holley maybe. Aw, wouldn't that be great?

STEVIE: Aw, yeah, Brett, jeez. And real wide mags, and spoilers, and flared guards, and custom paint, aw yeah, wait till we get out in that, eh, all the stuff we can do.

BRETT: Yeah, a car a man'd be proud to be seen in, cruisin' up the freeway, burnin' a bit of rubber, you know, outside the hospital.

GLENN: How you goin' to pay for it, but, mate?

BRETT: There's the money from gaol, plus the money you gave me. Use it to make a fresh start, you said, well that's exactly what I'm goin' to do.

GLENN: That'd only be a few hundred.

BRETT: Might not even need all of that. Those car salesman blokes, they're always ready to do a deal, frantic to arrange finance if you talk to 'em right.

STEVIE: Yeah, yeah, let's do it, eh? Hey, maybe even somethin' runnin' nitro, eh, wouldn't that be great?

> BRETT *throws aside his can and moves away.* STEVIE *follows eagerly, but* GLENN *hangs back uncertain.*

BRETT: Well, what are you waitin' for?

GLENN: Er, how was you thinkin' of gettin' there?

BRETT: Your car, of course.

GLENN: The Corolla?

BRETT: What do you reckon? Have you got a fuckin' Rolls Royce parked out there?

GLENN: I don't know about this, I mean, right at the moment, you know…

BRETT: You mean she won't let you.

GLENN: I'm not sayin' that. Stop givin' me shit about Jackie, alright?

BRETT: I just want to go and get meself a car, mate. You're me brother, and I need you to drive me. Is that too much to ask?

GLENN: Well, no, but…

STEVIE: S'pose we could get the bus.

BRETT: You're shitting me! Guys like us don't ride buses.

JACKIE *enters.*

JACKIE: What's going on?

BRETT: Yeah, mate, what's goin' on? You tell her straight, eh?

GLENN: We're just going out for a while, that's all. Me and me brothers. Brett wants to buy a car.

JACKIE: What, now?

BRETT: When do you think, next Christmas?

JACKIE: I thought we were going to have a barbecue.

GLENN: We just want to get this settled first, that's all. Brett's real keen. Won't take long.

JACKIE: But I've just put the dressing on the salads. They'll go limp.

GLENN: Ah, bugger the salads.

JACKIE: Well, that's nice. You asked me to make that dressing specially, because you liked it so much. Mustard, cream and fresh herbs.

BRETT: [*laughing*] Poor bastard! I reckon the salads aren't the only thing goin' limp round here.

GLENN: Look, we'll be quick, alright?

BRETT: Jesus, mate, do what you want to do. It's your car too, isn't it?

JACKIE: It isn't, actually. I mean, I didn't want to mention that, but seeing as you've asked, no it isn't.

BRETT: I thought you'd traded your wheels on it.

GLENN: Well, yeah, I did, but you know, I owed a fair bit, and Jackie sort of ended up payin' for most of it in the end.

BRETT: Jesus, that's what happens when the bitches start earnin' money. So now you got no rights at all, have you?

GLENN: 'Course I got rights. Look, stop makin' a big deal of things. [*To* JACKIE] Look, we're goin' out for a bit, okay?

JACKIE: Alright. Do what you want to do.

BRETT: Good on you, mate. You really laid down the law to her. Iron-fisted Glenn, that's the boy.

> GLENN *turns angrily to* BRETT.

GLENN: Just get off my back, will ya? Let's just go and get this over with, for Christ's sake.

> GLENN *downs his drink then throws away the can.* NOLA *enters, followed by* SANDRA.

NOLA: Stevie.

STEVIE: Aw, now what?

NOLA: I'm not feeling good. I feel awful.

STEVIE: Not again. Jesus.

NOLA: I'm sorry, but I can't help it. I keep feeling dizzy, and my tummy goes funny, and… I'm frightened, Stevie.

STEVIE: Why tell me? What can I do?

SANDRA: I think you better take her to the hospital, love.

STEVIE: Can't she get the bus?

JACKIE: Don't worry, I'll drive her.

BRETT: Hey, come on, we got the car.

JACKIE: This girl's pregnant and she's feeling sick. She needs to go to hospital.

STEVIE: She's always feelin' sick.

NOLA: I can't help it.

GLENN: Suppose we better let 'em go, then. What a bugger, eh?

BRETT: Yeah, that's right, just fold up and let 'em trample all over you. Evil it is, fuckin' evil. [*To* MICHELLE] You want to go with 'em?

MICHELLE: Me? Why?

BRETT: Be all of youse chicks together, won't it? You can swap stories about breakin' blokes' balls.

MICHELLE: I came here to be with you.

SANDRA: Go along with them, Stevie.

STEVIE: No!

SANDRA: You're in this with her. Aren't you man enough to see that?

STEVIE: I want to go with me brothers.

JACKIE: [*exasperated, to* STEVIE] Oh, grow a brain!

STEVIE: [*losing control*] One of these days you're not going to be able to make me do stuff no more, you know that? None of youse are, so stuff you! [*Near tears*] I'm not goin' to do nothin' I don't want to do no more. Nothin'! It'll be what I want to do what counts.

SANDRA: Go on, Stevie, off you go. That's a good kid.

STEVIE: No! Get lost!

SANDRA: Stevie! I'm not giving you any choice.

STEVIE: Aw, alright.

JACKIE: Let's go, then, for God's sake.

STEVIE: Wasn't like this before. Before all these others come along and spoiled it. Was just me and me brothers doin' whatever we wanted to do.

> JACKIE, NOLA *and* STEVIE *leave. Soon after there are the sounds of car doors shutting, an engine starting, and a car moving away.*

BRETT: Shit, you really stuffed that up, didn't you? No fuckin' car! Around this shit hole, you got no car, you got nothin'.

GLENN: Aw, what was I supposed to do? Be reasonable.

BRETT: Nah, fuck bein' reasonable. Had that. Alright, then, come on, we'll have to bloody hitch or somethin'.

GLENN: Alright.

MICHELLE: Hey, can I come too?

BRETT: What do you think this is, bush week? Don't want no chicks round when I'm tryin' to buy a car. Don't want them slimy salesman bastards thinkin' I'm soft. You give 'em an inch, they'll have your balls. You stay here and keep me mum company. See youse later.

SANDRA: Bye bye, love. You calm down and try and enjoy yourself. Get somethin' real nice, I reckon you deserve it.

GLENN: See you later, then.

> BRETT *and* GLENN *leave.* MICHELLE *sits down.*

SANDRA: Brett and cars. Now there's a recipe for disaster.

MICHELLE: Looks like the party's over before it even got started.

SANDRA: Well, Brett's got a few things to sort out.

MICHELLE: Bit hard to take. He bawls me out for keeping him waiting thirty seconds, then he forgets I'm even here.

SANDRA: Oh no, you're number one in Brett's life, don't you worry about that.

MICHELLE: Suppose you know him best. I'd have given up on him already if it hadn't been for you.

SANDRA: All men are like that, love, as far as I can tell. All they can see is what's in front of them. They don't seem to be able to look at what's underneath things. It's like they spend the whole time staring down the little cardboard tube from the middle of the Glad Wrap.

MICHELLE: Yeah.

SANDRA: All you can do is be patient, that's all. Take comfort from knowing that while they're out there doing what they're doing, they're probably thinking about you. At least some of the time.

Blackout.

END OF ACT ONE

ACT TWO

SCENE ONE

Lights up on the backyard. Monday, early evening. GLENN *and* BRETT *wrestle together on the ground, fighting furiously and spitefully. They are so entwined that neither can break free to land a blow. Instead they roll back and forth, grunting and snarling in anger.* SANDRA *sits up on the cane lounge, alarmed.*

SANDRA: Boys! Stop it!

> *The brawl goes on.* BRETT *begins to get the upper hand. He breaks one arm free and delivers a blow to* GLENN*'s head. He manages to get on top of* GLENN, *wrenching his arm behind his back and grinding his face into the dirt.* GLENN *groans in pain.*

BRETT: You want to take it back, do ya, you want to take it back?

GLENN: Bugger you!

> BRETT *pushes* GLENN *more heavily into the ground, wrenching at his arm, and digging a knee into his back*

SANDRA: Brett! Glenn! You behave!

BRETT: Nobody says what you said to me, pal, and gets away with it. I didn't spend a year in gaol to put up with that. Come on, take it back!

GLENN: I didn't mean nothin', but I got a right to me opinion. I'm not takin' nothin' back.

> BRETT *wrenches harder on* GLENN*'s arm, and grinds his face further into the dirt.*

Aw, Jesus, you're mad!

BRETT: Yeah, mate, I'm mad, I'm fuckin' furious! I spend half the mornin' bein' treated like shit by them creeps down Parramatta Road, and what do I get from you? Mockery and fuckin' ridicule. Smartarse!

GLENN: I can't help it if they wouldn't sell you a car. I mean, dressed like you was, couldn't you have at least kept your shirt on?

BRETT: I was hot, wasn't I?

GLENN: But then you tell them their cars are a heap of shit. What else are you going to get but a knockback?

BRETT: I got a short fuse, okay?

GLENN: Yeah, alright, but then you go and piss against that big cardboard cut-out of the dealer.

BRETT: Where else was there to go?

GLENN: Aw, Jesus.

BRETT: Fuck 'em. Nobody's puttin' nothin' over me, and nobody's givin' me a hard time and gettin' away with it! Least of all you! Come on, you goin' to take back what you said, or am I goin' to have to break every bone in your body?

> BRETT *attacks* GLENN *with a new burst of fury.* GLENN *cries out in pain.*

GLENN: Alright, alright! Jesus! I'm sorry, I didn't mean nothin'.

BRETT: You take it back, do ya? You take it back?

GLENN: Yeah. Yeah. Alright. I take it back. Yeah.

BRETT: You'll know better next time, won't you?

> BRETT *lets* GLENN *up, giving him a final whack to the head as he does so. He stands, then looks suddenly over the fence. He calls out.*

And what are you starin' at?

SANDRA: Now look what you've done, you've upset Mrs Purvis.

> BRETT *waves his fist towards the unseen onlooker.*

BRETT: Yah, piss off, you old bag, or I'll come round and give you one!

SANDRA: I'm ashamed of you boys! Both of you. Do you want people to think you're just hooligans who can't behave properly in your own home?

BRETT: I don't care what anybody thinks.

GLENN: I didn't mean nothin', it was just a joke, you know?

BRETT: Yeah? Didn't sound like it.

SANDRA: What joke?

BRETT: Yah, after I'd been gettin' the shaft from all these stinkin' mongrel car salesmen types, just as we're comin' home, round the corner here there's this little kiddie car thing, shaped like an elephant, and it's got these stupid ears that flap up and down when the wheels go round. Only it's all busted, and lyin' on its side, now, you know, had it. And this bastard, knowin' the state I'm in after all I just been through, says, 'Maybe you could afford that'. Jesus, mate, if you wasn't me brother, I'd have killed you!

> BRETT *gets himself a beer can, rips the top off and takes a swig.* GLENN *drags himself up onto a seat, and sits panting.* BRETT *throws him a can, which he catches, clumsily.*

Here, suck on this.

> GLENN *opens his can and begins drinking.*

SANDRA: I think you boys had something like that, didn't you? Only yours was a great big pelican, and its beak used to open and shut, it made this sort of gulping noise when you pedalled it. Aw, Stevie used to love that. [*Pause.*] So you didn't get a car. Well, that's a real shame.

BRETT: Nah. Seems I'm not a good credit risk, can you believe that? Jesus, why should those buggers care, it's the finance company's problem, not theirs.

GLENN: But you went straight for the muscle cars. I mean those Brock Commodores and that, they're askin' thirty grand or more. If you'd gone for somethin' a bit sensible, maybe you'd have had a chance.

BRETT: Sensible? Aw, yeah? Sensible? What, like a Corolla? [*Sneering*] A girlie's car. A little girlie's car.

GLENN: Aw, come on, you know what I mean.

BRETT: You never used a word like sensible before she come along. Got you by the balls, that bitch has.

GLENN: Look, stop sayin' that, will ya?

BRETT: She's got you by the balls! Jesus, if you was still any sort of a man you'd have backed me up, instead of lurkin' round like you was ashamed. You know, actually done somethin' to help, like offerin' to trade her stupid Corolla in and come into somethin' with me. Somethin' a bloke wouldn't be ashamed to be seen drivin'.

GLENN: Aw, you know there's reasons why I couldn't do that.

BRETT: Yeah, that's exactly what I'm talkin about.

SANDRA: Boys, will you stop all this? All this bickering and fighting. You've always been best mates.

BRETT: Things have changed, I reckon.

GLENN: Yeah, pity you can't face up to that. Try and accept, your little brother's got his own life to lead now, he doesn't have to run round doin' what you want.

BRETT: Looks to me like you're goin' out of your way not to do anythin' I want.

GLENN: That just isn't true.

BRETT: Yeah?

SANDRA: Oh, Brett. Glenn. Don't throw it all away. What we had. There were times when about the only good thing you could say about this family was that we were together. But, by gee, we did that well. Whatever anybody else said, to each other, we mattered.

GLENN: I'm not sayin' Brett doesn't matter to me. I'm sayin' I wish he'd stop givin' me the shits.

BRETT: Hah.

The sound of a car arriving outside. Doors slamming.

Hey, here's your boss.

GLENN: Don't say that stuff while she's here.

BRETT: I'll say what I want to say, mate. Always have, always will.

JACKIE enters, followed by NOLA and STEVIE.

SANDRA: Everything okay, love?

JACKIE: Nothing that can't be fixed with a bit of rest and a bit of TLC.

SANDRA: Well, that's good to hear, anyway.

NOLA: They told me I'm doing everything wrong.

JACKIE: They weren't criticising you. They were just saying you've got to lie down more.

SANDRA: That sounds like good advice, anyway.

JACKIE: They say that with her medical history she's got to take special care, no more stress, no more being shouted at and pushed around. Otherwise she may lose the baby.

NOLA: Stop talking like I wasn't here. She this and she that.

SANDRA: Jackie's only trying to help, Nola.

JACKIE: I'm glad somebody can see that.

NOLA: Just 'cause she knows how hospitals work, and doctors and all that, and we don't, doesn't give her the right to treat me and Stevie the way she did, orderin' us around like dickheads.

JACKIE gives a sigh of exaggerated despair.

JACKIE: Oh, why do I even bother?

BRETT: Aw, all this women's talk. Jesus, I've had enough of it. [*He moves away, then stops, his attention suddenly taken by something next door.*] Aw, are you gawkin' at us again, you stupid ugly old bag? Alright, you want some action, cop an eyeful of this.

BRETT *turns around and drops his jeans, bending over to bare his bottom to the onlooker.*

JACKIE: Oh, that's really charming.

SANDRA: Brett, don't be disgusting.

BRETT: Yah! Frustrated old cow. [*He pulls up his jeans and turns to go inside. Then he waves back in the direction of Mrs Purvis and calls out.*] Hey, I'm goin' to go inside now, goin' to get me conjugal rights from me woman. You want to come and watch, dogface?

SANDRA: You've gone too far, Brett. The poor old dear never hurt anyone.

BRETT *leaves.*

STEVIE: [*laughing*] Hah, that showed the old bag a thing or two, didn't it?

JACKIE: Yes, yes, very clever. Very amusing.

GLENN: [*to* JACKIE] Hey, look, just lay off my family, will you?

JACKIE: To be honest, I've had some members of your family up to here. This one refusing to even try to understand that the doctor wasn't criticising her. And this one [*indicating* STEVIE] going on about how it's not fair, and trying to run away all the time. Oh, it was great fun, I can tell you.

GLENN: Running away?

STEVIE: I didn't, I just went for a walk.

JACKIE: In the middle of a crowded waiting room he starts shouting at Nola, about her ruining his life. Then he goes running off down the corridor, crashing into people. Knocked over some poor old man on crutches. And when I found him he was sitting under a tree, swearing his head off like a cranky little boy.

SANDRA: Were you a bit upset, Stevie, love?

STEVIE: Yeah, yeah, I fuckin' was. Fuckin' am. It's all giving me the shits.

JACKIE: Yeah, and me. And if that's the way you feel, just don't go expecting me ever to do anything to help this family again.

GLENN: What do you want, a fuckin' medal? So you drove 'em somewhere. Great. Thanks a lot. Doesn't mean you can just go riding roughshod all the time with that sharp tongue of yours. Other people got feelings too, you know.

STEVIE: Yeah, you tell her, Glenn, you tell her what's what.

GLENN: Aw, shut up, Stevie, will ya. Just go away or somethin'.

STEVIE: Eh? Me?

> SANDRA *stands, with some difficulty.*

SANDRA: Yes, come on, Stevie love. Let's go inside and have a cup of tea. And you too, Nola, would you like that?

NOLA: Don't know. S'pose.

SANDRA: Yes, let's leave them to it. Looks like they've got private things to say to each other.

GLENN: Too fuckin' right.

NOLA: Time somebody told her off, anyway. See how she likes it.

> SANDRA, STEVIE *and* NOLA *leave.*

GLENN: I'm trying to tell you something, alright? Why don't you try fuckin' listening for a change?

JACKIE: Don't swear at me. I'm sick of all the swearing that goes on around here.

GLENN: Are ya? Are ya, eh? Well, you'll have to fuckin' put up with it, 'cause we're not going to change.

JACKIE: No, I can see that.

GLENN: That's what you want, isn't it? For us to be somethin' different. Me especially.

JACKIE: Well, I thought you wanted that too.

GLENN: There's things I want out of life. Better things than I been used to. But that doesn't mean I'm goin' to turn me back on me family and kick 'em in the teeth. Whatever you might think, however things might look to you. This is where I come from, okay? They're me.

JACKIE: Alright then. Maybe you should come back here. Move your things out of the flat. Is that what you want?

GLENN: I'm not sayin' that. Jesus, do you have to get everything round the wrong way all the time? I sometimes think you do it deliberate.

JACKIE: I'd just like to know what you want. I don't think that's too much to ask.

GLENN: I've been tryin' to tell you, haven't I? Stop pourin' shit on me family.

> GLENN *throws away his empty can, and reaches for another one. He opens it and takes swig.*

JACKIE: I wish you'd lay off that stuff a bit.

GLENN: Yeah, you reckon?

JACKIE: For one thing you're getting a beer gut. I don't like being seen around with a man who doesn't look after himself.

GLENN: I put on a couple of kilos, that's all. That's normal.

JACKIE: You used to be really trim. Sort of athletic. I liked that a lot. But now, you don't come jogging with me anymore, and you don't do your push-ups. And you guzzle that stuff all the time.

GLENN: Yeah, well, I got me reasons.

JACKIE: I thought we had a good thing going, being together.

GLENN: Yeah, we do, okay, I'm not sayin' we don't.

JACKIE: You know, I liked you because I thought you were like me. You've got a lot of life in you, real potential to make something of yourself.

GLENN: Just like you, eh?

JACKIE: I'd look at you sometimes, when we were out somewhere, I'd see the look on your face. And I could tell, you were sizing things up, taking it all in, making sure you knew what all the rules were before you jumped in and took them on. Sort of thoughtful, and deliberate. Someone who makes things happen properly.

GLENN: Yeah, well, maybe I am like that a bit.

JACKIE: And I thought we could help each other get through, end up with something to show for it all. I mean, you've seen where I come from, I've got no more right to put on airs than you have. But we're both entitled to a bit of self respect, don't you think?

GLENN: Yeah, alright, of course we are.

JACKIE: Only that doesn't fall out of the sky because you want it to. You've got to earn it. You've got to act so you deserve it.

GLENN: You reckon?

JACKIE: Yeah. And that's why I find what goes on around here so hard to take. That's why I get so cross. Not because of what they're like, but because of what happens to you.

GLENN: It's difficult here sometimes. You've got to understand that. Especially with Brett. And I'm asking for a bit of support from you, not sniping away and bossing everybody around. That only makes things ten times worse.

JACKIE: Well, I'm like that.

GLENN *goes over to the car seat and sits down. He takes a drink.*

GLENN: I don't know, at the start of things with us, it was me that wanted to keep me distance from this place, and you that wanted to be part of the family.

JACKIE: I'd never really known what it was like to be part of a family before. For a while I thought I could. You can't say I didn't try.

GLENN: No, I got to give you that.

JACKIE: I even wanted to visit Brett in gaol. But you stopped me. Hey, can I have a sip of that?

She sits down next to GLENN. *He passes her the can. She drinks.*

GLENN: Yeah, didn't want him to scare you off. Didn't want to lose you, I s'pose. Still don't.

JACKIE *places a hand on* GLENN*'s knee.*

JACKIE: I don't want to lose you, either.

GLENN: You'll do me, I reckon, Jackie. Most of the time, anyway.

They kiss.

JACKIE: Why don't we just go home? Leave them to it.

GLENN *pulls back amazed.*

GLENN: What?

JACKIE: Things will only get worse here today. Brett will get wilder and Stevie will get more and more stupid and pathetic.

GLENN *stands up angrily, confronting* JACKIE.

GLENN: You're talkin' about me brothers!

JACKIE: You know I'm telling the truth.

GLENN: They're my brothers, alright, and they're me best mates and they always will be, and no stupid fuckin' woman could ever understand that in a million years.

JACKIE: What do you mean they're your mates? They give you the shits most of the time.

GLENN: So what if they do? Mates are mates! So just shut up, alright! Shut up!

JACKIE *pulls back. Blackout.*

SCENE TWO

Weeks later. The living room. It is evening. SANDRA *is lying on the cane lounge.* MICHELLE *sits nearby. They are watching television.*

MICHELLE: I'm turning that off, Sandra. I'm not watching any more.

SANDRA: Yeah, go ahead. I've seen it five times already.

MICHELLE: Doesn't tell you anything, the TV. Doesn't show you what those people were really like. When they led Brett out of the van and up the steps. Jeez, if the cops hadn't had their guns and their dogs, those people would have made mincemeat out of Brett.

SANDRA: Yeah, he doesn't look in much of a state to defend himself, does he, after all those weeks on the run. Nothing but a skeleton. Probably hasn't had a square meal since he left here.

MICHELLE: And if that mob had caught up with me, I'd have been the one who was mincemeat. They must have figured out who I was from the way that reporter was pesterin' me. Suddenly I was it. And, you know, Brett and the others, they've been charged with somethin', so you can sort of understand it, but me, what am I supposed to have done? I had to run for me life, you know, I mean for real. God, what chance will the boys have?

SANDRA: I don't know. I'm starting to wonder.

MICHELLE *picks up a tabloid newspaper from the table.*

MICHELLE: All this stuff. The coroner's report, and all the details of what happened, and those pictures of the boys that make them look like the worst crims you ever seen. They don't look like that. No-one looks like that. [*Pause.*] Whatever happened to that girl. However terrible it was. It wasn't the boys who did it.

SANDRA: No, of course it wasn't. Of course it wasn't.

MICHELLE: It just wasn't. I know. However bad it might look. Whatever evidence they might think they've come up with. Seems like they want to make people imagine 'em doing it. This stupid drawing, with all the arrows going from McDonalds to the junkyard, and the drain, and where they found the car. Where they found the clothes. Where they found…

Pause.

SANDRA: Where they found the body.

MICHELLE: Yes. [*Pause.*] That's why those pictures of the boys are like that. Like no-one has ever looked. Because they want people to think to themselves, 'It's only scum who do things like that, not decent ordinary people like me'.

SANDRA: My boys are decent ordinary boys.

MICHELLE: No, there's something weird going on with all this. Like something's gone wild, out of control. And they think the only way they can stop it is to take everything out on Brett and the boys. This wild thing that's happening now, they think the boys are it, so they want to destroy them. Like if they wipe them off the face of the earth, life'll go back to how it used to be.

> NOLA *enters, slowly, almost as if in a trance. She is more noticeably pregnant than before.*

SANDRA: You alright, Nola love?

NOLA: No, I keep thinking about what those blokes in the gaol did to Stevie.

SANDRA: I know, it was terrible.

NOLA: I've been lying in there having sort of dreams, even when I'm awake. I keep seein' Stevie flyin' through the air and crashin' down, and feet goin' into him, and him yellin' and cryin' and gettin' up, and them doin' it to him again and again and again. And I keep feelin' it myself, and I can't stand it, I want to be with him, not here on me own. I want him around.

SANDRA: Well, we're around, anyway. I know it's not like having him, but we'll do our best.

MICHELLE: Yes, we'll do what we can, we're all in this together.

NOLA: I wish I could just go to sleep, and not dream or anything. Just wake up when all this is over. Or not wake up at all, eh, maybe that'd be even better.

MICHELLE: No, you can't let them beat you like that.

NOLA: But they have already, haven't they? What's the point of pretending?

> NOLA *leaves.*

SANDRA: Poor girl. Hard for her to find much to cling to.

MICHELLE: Yeah. Hasn't got much to show for it all, has she? I mean, the rest of us, at least we've knocked around a bit, had a bit of excitement, a bit of joy, so we can at least say, well, that's the way it goes. But Nola. No, there's nothing she can say to herself that makes this any easier to look at.

SANDRA: So it's up to us. To give her what strength we've got.

MICHELLE: Yeah. Yeah, you're right.

SANDRA: That's what you do it for, isn't it? The only reason you go through it all, all the daily effort and all the love you put into bringing them up. So at the end, you can still say, some of the time, we were alright together.

MICHELLE: And you did pretty well, too, Sandra, judging by some of the things Brett's told me.

SANDRA: Did he say that?

MICHELLE: Yes.

SANDRA: Once Les had gone his own way, I was their guidin' light. Any goodness in 'em, they had to get from me. Was no-one else.

MICHELLE: No.

SANDRA: Those boys are my life! They're the only life I've got. [*She is almost overcome.*] So it's like those people are stickin' daggers into me, believin' what they believe. Christ, if that was really true what they say, I couldn't go on. I'd go out of my mind.

> JACKIE *enters. She is dressed in a coat with the collar turned up high, and has a scarf over her head, and sunglasses, as if trying to avoid being detected. She is carrying an overnight bag.*

JACKIE: Alright, here I am, see. I've come crawling back, do you want to gloat over it a bit, do you, rub it in a bit?

SANDRA: Nobody around here wants to do any gloating.

MICHELLE: Suppose you heard that Brett's caught.

JACKIE: He made quite a splash.

MICHELLE: Yeah, real TV star. So now they got 'em all. You manage to get in to see Glenn?

JACKIE: No.

MICHELLE: No, Nola couldn't get in to see Stevie, either, after he got bashed up. They said it was for security reasons. What did they tell you?

JACKIE: Oh, nothing really.

MICHELLE: What, didn't you try?

JACKIE: Yes, of course I did.

MICHELLE: Huh, doesn't sound like it.

JACKIE: Look, don't start that stuff again, making out I don't care. I made enquiries, there was nothing I could do, alright?

MICHELLE: I went to the court to try and see Brett. Just to get a glimpse. And if I'd thought there was a chance of talkin' to him I'd have clawed through the walls with my fingernails, that's how much it mattered to me.

JACKIE: Well, hooray for you.

MICHELLE: I hung around, what's more, put me neck at risk from that mob snarlin' and yellin' outside.

JACKIE: You can't blame them, can you, after what happened to that girl?

MICHELLE: Yeah. Yeah, you can blame them. When they're trying to put it onto blokes that are innocent. Don't you agree? [*Pause.*] Well, don't you? Don't you think that however bad it was, what was done to that girl, it's wrong they should try and string up blokes when they haven't even proved they did it?

JACKIE: Yes, alright, of course I think that's wrong.

SANDRA: Of course she does, love, she's still one of us.

MICHELLE: I just can't figure you out, that's the problem. I just don't reckon you're acting like any normal person would.

JACKIE: Maybe you should take the trouble to find out what's been happening. To me.

MICHELLE: Yeah?

JACKIE: Yeah. You talk about having had that mob chasing after you outside the court. I had them in my flat.

MICHELLE: You what?

JACKIE: Two nights ago. When that coroner's report came out. After the newspapers and the TV had been going all day about those disgusting, evil things that were done, some of the neighbours just went berserk. They came in like a cyclone and tore the place apart. They spat at me, and swore, but then they let me run for it. But, aw, what they did then. The filthy, obscene things they wrote on the walls. And somebody did a... [*Pause.*] Somebody did a shit on the floor.

MICHELLE: That's rough, I got to admit.

JACKIE: Then I went to the police. And can you believe it, they laughed at me. They said what did I expect, hanging round with blokes like that. One of them said, 'Serves you right, you slut, pity the boys didn't work you over instead of that poor girl'. Then he pushed me up against the wall and started putting his hands all over me and…

JACKIE breaks down. MICHELLE *puts a hand on her shoulder.*

SANDRA: They're having a field day, aren't they?

JACKIE: I spent the night at a motel. Couldn't possibly go home. And all night, I just imagined being that poor girl, went through all the different things that must have happened over those hours. I just couldn't stop. I saw them, and felt them, all those things they were doing, heard all the words they must have been saying. All the filth and hatred they let loose on women, where does it come from?

MICHELLE *pulls back.*

MICHELLE: Who were you imagining, but?

JACKIE: Why do they hate us so much?

MICHELLE: Not the boys, you weren't imagining the boys?

JACKIE: And by the morning, I was feeling all bruised and aching. Hadn't slept a wink. Went off to work like I was in a trance.

MICHELLE: Work? You went to work? You mean they'd still have you?

JACKIE: My boss has been really nice. Through the whole thing. Kept saying I was one of his most valued employees and he didn't care what anyone else thought. But halfway through the morning, this really dignified guy in a suit, he recognises me. He says, 'You're the girlfriend of that maniac rapist killer Glenn Sprague, you ought to be strung up with the rest of them'. [*Pause.*] Then I suppose I sort of exploded. I jumped over the counter and hit him and scratched at him and screamed and screamed and screamed.

SANDRA: Well, good on you.

MICHELLE: Yes, didn't think you had it in you, to be honest.

JACKIE: So now I don't have a job, and I don't have a home, and I don't have any standing in the community anymore, any respect. I'm on my own.

MICHELLE: Join the club.

JACKIE: Why did it have to happen like this? Why?

SANDRA: Well, that's a question we'd all like an answer to, love.

MICHELLE: Yeah, but don't hold your breath.

JACKIE: Why now? Why here?

MICHELLE: Anywhere but where you are, eh?

JACKIE: Yes! If you want to put it like that. Yes. I'm a decent girl who's always tried her hardest to make life alright. And I deserve better than what I got mixed up with by coming here.

MICHELLE: Then why the hell are you here?

JACKIE: [*angry*] Because I've got nowhere else to go! [*Pause.*] I've got nowhere else to go.

SANDRA: Like I said before, you're part of the family, so you're welcome here, whatever you might have said in the heat of the moment. Isn't that right, Michelle?

MICHELLE: No. I'll tell you straight. I don't want to have anything to do with her. Until such time as she comes right out and says to me, no hedging around, no pulling back, but comes straight out with it and says, 'I don't think the boys did it'. Nothing else'll do.

JACKIE: I can't say that. I wish I could, but I can't. I just don't know.

MICHELLE: Yeah, well, there's a lot of things I don't know either, but I know what I believe.

JACKIE: But I told you, I keep imagining all the things that were done to that girl before she finally died. And I keep remembering some of the things that were going on here. Some of the things that were said. And I can't help suspecting, I just can't help it.

MICHELLE: We're talking about the blokes we love. Doesn't that mean anything to you?

JACKIE: Well yes, but…

MICHELLE: It means a hell of a lot to me! Me and Brett. What we are. That might not be much in some people's eyes, but I'll tell you. My love for Brett, that's kind of like, part of what I am. How I operate. Part of how I get through the day. And I'm not giving that up without a fight, I'm bloody not, whatever he's…

Pause.

JACKIE: Go on, say it. Whatever he's done.

MICHELLE: No. That isn't what I mean. You know it isn't.

JACKIE: I'd like to believe you, you know. I wish it was that easy.

MICHELLE: It's not easy! Of course it isn't. But it's the only thing you can do if the love you have's worth anything! And if you can't take that step and see things the way I'm talking about, then I don't want to be anywhere near you.

JACKIE: I'm sorry, I really am, but...

MICHELLE: I mean it's up to you, Sandra. If you want to throw me out and have her stay here instead, well, I can't stop you, but one of us will have to go.

SANDRA: I wouldn't throw you out, Michelle. What do you think I am? You've stood by me through thick and thin.

JACKIE: I'd go somewhere else if I could. I tried. But I couldn't survive another night in a motel, I couldn't, I'd go insane, really insane. And none of my friends will have anything to do with me anymore, so...

MICHELLE: So we're all there is left.

JACKIE: Yes.

MICHELLE: So do what you got to do, then. Why keep messing around?

Pause. JACKIE *paces around the room. The others watch.*

JACKIE: I'd like to see things the way you do. I'd like to think that the boys went off to a mate's place and drank for a few hours and then sort of passed out. And when this thing happened, the police thought, well, those Sprague brothers have been letting off a bit of steam lately, disturbing the peace a bit, let's put it on them.

MICHELLE: You're doing well, Jackie. You're doing real well.

SANDRA: Yes, keep it up, love. We all got to hear this as often as we can.

JACKIE: And those things they called evidence. Stevie having cuts and bruises all over him, and mud. Well, we all know how clumsy poor little Stevie can be, he probably did fall into a drain when he was walking home drunk.

MICHELLE: Yes, of course he did.

JACKIE: And the reason Glenn didn't turn up for work that morning, well, Glenn's no dummy, he would have figured the police might try and pin it on him. And he didn't want to make a big scene at work, and embarrass me. He was thinking of me.

MICHELLE: Right. Of course he'd think of you.

JACKIE: And as for your Brett. Well, talk about give a dog a bad name. Just out of gaol, so right away they try to get him for something he didn't do. So he'd have said to himself, 'No, the system doesn't work for a man like me, I'll have to go undercover until I can clear my name. Become an outlaw, like Ned Kelly.'

MICHELLE: Now you're getting it. You're not such a bad bitch after all, are you?

JACKIE: And somewhere out there are the blokes that really did it. And they're psychopaths, criminally insane, freaks of nature, that's what they are, they're nothing at all like Stevie, Glenn and Brett.

MICHELLE: You can stay. You might have started off trying to lie, but I can tell by the way you're talking, you've come round to believing it just as much as the rest of us.

Pause. JACKIE *sits down, suddenly exhausted.*

JACKIE: Thank you.

NOLA *enters holding her stomach, distressed.*

NOLA: I think something's happening! [*She is jolted by a contraction.*] Oh! A contraction maybe. But how are you supposed to know if it is?

SANDRA: Come here, love.

SANDRA *sits up on the couch.* NOLA *comes over. On the way she is jolted by another contraction.*

NOLA: Oh! They keep getting bigger and bigger.

SANDRA: Give us a look at your watch, Jackie. I think I remember something about them being two minutes apart when the baby's coming.

She holds a hand on NOLA*'s stomach and looks at the watch.* NOLA *is jolted by a further contraction.*

Or maybe it's only supposed to be one minute.

NOLA: Aw! Here it comes again! It's like nothing you could ever imagine! It's everywhere!

MICHELLE *puts an arm around* NOLA *as the next contraction comes on.*

MICHELLE: How long was that one, Sandra?

SANDRA: Maybe it's supposed to be half a minute!

NOLA: Oh, what am I going to do?

They wait, looking anxiously at the watch. Further contractions come.

SANDRA: Twenty seconds.

JACKIE: Never mind the watch. It's just one big contraction.

NOLA: I'm scared.

SANDRA: Don't be, love. This is the one thing they can't take away from you, whatever else they do.

MICHELLE: Looks like we'd better get you to a hospital. [*To* JACKIE] Can I borrow your keys? I'll drive her.

JACKIE: No, let's all go. Together.

> *Blackout.*

SCENE THREE

Monday evening. The backyard. BRETT *stands defiantly, looking off towards the driveway.* GLENN, STEVIE *and* NOLA *are in the background.* BRETT *waves two fingers as the sound of a car diminishes.*

BRETT: Fuckin' cops! Chargin' into a bloke's welcome home party just because he's bared his bum to some ugly old bag. Christ, it's only natural, lettin' off a bit of steam.

STEVIE: Yeah, scum, they are.

BRETT: Bargin' right into the bedroom when a bloke's in there with his woman. Jesus, I'm so angry I could kill!

STEVIE: Yeah, you'd pulverise 'em, mate. We all would.

BRETT: Talkin' to me like that. Who do they bloody think they are?

STEVIE: Yeah, gives you the shits, doesn't it?

BRETT: Those pigs. Big-time. Tough guys. Aw, yeah, let's see 'em without their uniforms and their guns. Down a back alley some time. Let's see how tough they are then!

GLENN: Look, calm down, mate, for Christ's sake.

BRETT: Don't tell me to calm down! What's the point of calmin' down when life's like this? About the only reasonable thing you can do is get mad!

> BRETT *takes a beer can from the carton, and goes into the house.* GLENN *takes a can, opens it, and moves away. He sits down and begins drinking.*

STEVIE: [*to* NOLA] Aw, alright, do you have to sit there bein' sulky all the time?

NOLA: What am I supposed to do after all that?

STEVIE: Just stop givin' me the shits, alright?

NOLA: Havin' to listen to all those things the cops were sayin' about me. And you. Knowin' half of 'em were true.

STEVIE: Aw, bullshit they were. That's just the sort of stuff people always say about us.

NOLA: They're right, but. I don't know what I'm goin' to do with this kid, I got no idea, and neither have you.

STEVIE: Aw, don't give me that stuff again. I mean, it's not my fault, I never wanted a kid, or you, or nothin'.

NOLA: Yeah, but the kid's goin' to be here, and there's nothin' any of us can do to make it go away.

STEVIE: Well, if there's nothin' any of us can do, then why go on and on whingein' about it all the time? Why don't you just leave me alone?

NOLA: 'Cause I'm hurtin' after all those things the cops said. About how I should be.

STEVIE: Aw, yeah, but they don't know nothin'.

NOLA: And you do, I suppose.

STEVIE: More than them cops, yeah. Bugger 'em.

NOLA: When that squinty lookin' one says to me, 'You ought to be a bit more choosy about the sort of bloke you get mixed up with', I thought to meself, 'Yeah, I should have been, shouldn't I?', but I couldn't go on waiting. And when he says, 'What chance is this kid of yours goin' to have bein' brought up in a place where men go round exposin' 'emselves to the neighbours?' I thought, 'Yeah, what chance?' But it's not goin' to have any choice, is it?

STEVIE: Yeah, it's got a choice. Same as you have. Piss off, like I been tellin' you for months, just piss off.

NOLA: But I can't, now, you made it so I can't. You kind of took me over.

STEVIE: Aw, I did not, you're just makin' it up. Just 'cause of one night in the back of the car.

NOLA: But you said things to me then, like you wanted me around.

STEVIE: Jesus, don't you know nothin'? A bloke can't help some of the things he says when he's, you know, doin' it. But those things don't mean nothin' afterwards, and shit, if you was any sort of woman you'd have known that.

NOLA: But you made it happen. You kept followin' me round, beggin' me to get into the car. You must have wanted me.

STEVIE: You was the only one left, that's all. All the other chicks out there had been taken. What's a bloke supposed to do? I couldn't help it. And when you was in the back of the car, and I was doin' it to you, I wasn't even thinkin' about you. So there, eh, what do you reckon about that?

NOLA: Well, if that's true, it's not your baby then, 'cause you don't deserve it!

> NOLA *bursts into tears and runs back into the house.* STEVIE *approaches* GLENN.

STEVIE: Jesus, what's a bloke supposed to do, eh? They go on and on with this stupid romantic shit, and when you tell 'em the truth, they chuck wobblies all over the place.

GLENN: Yeah, we all got our problems, haven't we? And I reckon we all got more or less the same one.

STEVIE: Yeah, the bitches, what makes 'em think they're so special?

> JACKIE *enters.*

JACKIE: What have you done to that poor girl now? She's in there bawling her eyes out.

STEVIE: Nothin'! I haven't done nothin'!

JACKIE: All this stress could make her lose the baby.

STEVIE: Just leave me alone, will ya?

JACKIE: Not that you could care less, could you? You haven't got it in you to care.

> GLENN *stands up, angry.*

GLENN: [*shouting*] Leave him alone! You come out here and start pushin' Stevie around. Where were ya when the pigs were here, eh, hidin' under the bed?

> STEVIE *moves into the background.*

JACKIE: I thought the best thing to do was keep out of it. What was I supposed to have done?

GLENN: Shown some loyalty, that's what! Stood up and been counted. Suppose you're ashamed of us, are ya?

JACKIE: Yes, quite frankly, I am. And I don't know how you can talk about loyalty, after all the hurtful things you said to me before.

GLENN: Stiff shit!

JACKIE: I'm not going to put up with it anymore.

GLENN: No, you won't put up with nothin', will ya, you won't do nothin' anyone tells you, you won't even make an effort to go along with things a bit. Who the hell do you think you are, anyway?

JACKIE: The same person I've always been. I've got my own standards, my own way of going about things, and I'm not going to drop it all just for you.

GLENN: Yeah, that's your trouble, isn't it? You won't even try and understand.

JACKIE: I've tried, over and over again.

GLENN: Yeah? I bet you got no idea what it's been like for me, bein' with you. Havin' you doin' these things to help me get on in life, improve meself. How do you think I feel as a man, eh? You make me feel as if without you I'd be nothin' but a failure. You tryin' to break me balls, are ya?

JACKIE: Oh, for heaven's sake!

GLENN: You're not feminine, you know that? That's your problem. I mean, shit, when I think of some of the things you do. Like the way you get on top of me sometimes, in bed, I mean, okay, I sort of let you do it, but jeez, if you want me honest opinion, it's bloody disgustin', it is, it's not natural.

JACKIE: Please, do we have to talk about this sort of thing now?

GLENN: What, in front of me brother? I got no secrets from him. [*He calls out.*] Hey, Stevie, you ought to see her sometime, she bounces up and down on top of me like she was ridin' a horse, makes these little squeakin' noises, eek, eek, eek.

JACKIE: You're disgusting! You're just as low as the rest of them. I don't know why I thought you could be any different.

GLENN *moves aggressively at* JACKIE.

GLENN: Yeah? Yeah? Disgustin', am I? Disgustin'?

JACKIE *backs away.* GLENN *pulls back.* JACKIE *goes quickly into the house.*

STEVIE: Good on you, mate.

GLENN: Aww, what's the point? Got better things to do than sortin' her out.

BRETT *enters, drinking from a beer can.*

BRETT: Thought you was goin' to deck her there for a moment. Thought you'd finally come to your senses.

GLENN: Yah, not worth the trouble.

> MICHELLE *enters slowly, as if a little stunned, and gets herself a beer. She drinks.*

BRETT: You alright?

MICHELLE: Yeah, I'll be okay.

BRETT: I'm not goin' to apologise or nothin', if that's what you're after.

> GLENN *moves into the background with* STEVIE.

MICHELLE: No, I'm just sad.

BRETT: Just don't make a big deal out of it, alright?

MICHELLE: I understand, honestly. You're all wound up after what you've been through. You couldn't help lashing out at me.

BRETT: I don't even know whether me fist connected with you.

MICHELLE: Alright, yeah, best to put it behind us, eh? There's plenty of time to get things right again. Remember what it was like before? We'll get back to that.

BRETT: Will you just stop talkin' about it, for Christ's sake. Don't you think a bloke's got his feelings?

MICHELLE: But I've got mine too. And I thought I was sort of like a mate.

BRETT: I didn't crack onto you 'cause I wanted a mate! I got mates.

> BRETT *turns sharply away, joining his brothers.*

MICHELLE: I'll be in the house, Brett, if you decide you want to talk about it. I'll be waiting. Should be good at that by now, shouldn't I?

> MICHELLE *leaves.*

BRETT: Jesus! Women! [*He throws his empty can aside, then goes to the carton and reaches for another, but finds it's empty.*] Aw, great, we're out of piss.

STEVIE: Have some of this one, mate.

> STEVIE *eagerly offers* BRETT *his can.* BRETT *snatches it and takes a drink.*

BRETT: Thanks, but we got to get some more.

GLENN: What's wrong, mate? Your woman giving you trouble too?

BRETT: Yeah. Jesus, what's wrong with 'em, they're always poking round trying to find your soft side.

GLENN: Yeah, soft side, Jesus, what bullshit is that?

BRETT: I don't know, do they do it to spite you, or do they just not know any better? Awwgh! [*Angrier*] I could bloody go crazy if I don't get what I want! Come on, let's get down to that bottle shop, I want to get serious!

> JACKIE *enters and approaches* GLENN.

JACKIE: I've just come to tell you, I'm going home.

GLENN: I don't care what you do. Just give me the keys to the car, okay, we're goin' to pick up some grog.

JACKIE: You're joking. You think I'd let you drive the car in the state you're in? Any of you? I'm going in to collect my salad bowls, and then…

GLENN: Fuck your salad bowls. You can take your salad bowls and you can stick them right up your arse!

JACKIE: I'm going to collect my salad bowls, and then I'm going home. If you want to come by and collect your things, could you please ring first so I can be out?

> JACKIE *moves towards the house.*

GLENN: Hey, come on, I told you, just give me the keys!

JACKIE: No! If you want them, you'll have to knock me down and take them from me. Maybe you can ask your brothers to help.

> GLENN *takes a few paces after* JACKIE, *but pulls back.*

BRETT: Hey, you gutless wonder, are you just goin' to let her get away with that?

> JACKIE *leaves.*

GLENN: Yah, who needs the bitch?

BRETT: So, you finally woke up to yourself, have you? Well, about time, that's all I can say. Shit, it hurt to see what was happenin' to you. Me own brother.

GLENN: [*angry at* BRETT] You don't know what I've been through, mate. How could any man cope with what I been through with her? Women just aren't human, the stuff they do to ya.

STEVIE: Yeah, they destroy you, don't they, that's what they do, bitches.

BRETT: Why does any bloke bother when that's all he ends up with? This. You go runnin' after 'em, you go messin' up your whole life because of 'em. All because you want to fuck 'em, right?

GLENN: Yeah, that's about all the use they are.

BRETT: They think they got power over you because of what they got between their legs, as if that makes 'em worth somethin'. They ought to try bein' a bloke sometime. See how hard he has to work to be worth anythin'.

STEVIE: Yeah, it's real hard bein' a bloke.

BRETT: And then when you do it to them, it's not even like you get anythin' for your trouble.

GLENN: Nah. I mean, you want it to be a big deal, when you get real wound up, dyin' for it, but shit, you know even then, deep down, they're laughin' at ya. It's fuckin' criminal.

BRETT: Too right it is, yeah, it's not how it's supposed to be at all. I mean, you got a right, haven't you, you got a right to know it's nothin' but you that matters, while you're workin' her over. No other thought in her stupid little head, nothin' but, Jesus, this bloke fucks like a wild animal!

GLENN: Right, but did one of 'em ever give you that, ever? No way. Makes you feel like punchin' their lights out.

BRETT: I reckon that's about all you can do, too, if you want to come out of it with any self-respect left. I mean, there's a way a man deserves to feel, isn't there, by rights, like a soldier in a battle, he's fought and won? A fuckin' warrior in the olden days, conquering! A hero!

STEVIE: Yeah, too right, I want to feel like a hero!

BRETT: And that's what they ought to want from a bloke, too, awwgh, fuckin' domination and power, explodin' into 'em like a bomb goin' off!

GLENN: Yeah, my fuckin' oath that's what they want, whatever they tell you, with all those fuckin' lies fillin' up their heads. A woman's still a woman, whatever she might think.

BRETT: There's just one thing they need. [*To* GLENN] A bloke like you or me on top of 'em. Goin' for it!

STEVIE: Yeah, right. A bloke like me, too.

BRETT: Aw, I can just about feel her right now, under me. Awwgh, yeah, eh, some real classy bitch, the sort who'd cut you dead in the shoppin' mall if you tried to perv on her.

STEVIE: Yeah, I know the ones, the way they dress, eh, all silky blouses and that, big V down the front, tits practically hangin' out. Awwgh!

BRETT: And their legs, eh, all covered in that nylon stuff, and those dresses swishin'. Why do you reckon they wear that if they're not just beggin' for you to look right up 'em?

GLENN: Only if you do, they try to have you locked up.

BRETT: Hundreds of times, I could have had one of 'em right there, if she'd been honest with herself. Fuckin' spread her out and gone for it, made her scream for more.

GLENN: Yeah, at your mercy.

BRETT: Aw, why did we let 'em get away? We should have hunted 'em down like wild pigs!

GLENN: They're still out there, mate, don't you worry.

STEVIE: Aw, I want 'em, I want 'em!

GLENN: But what do we get stuck with, eh? Them in there.

BRETT: Yeah, trouble is, 'cause of what you're after, you got to have 'em hangin' round the rest of the time. You got to put up with all the rest of the things they do, all the stupid stuff they come out with, and jeez does it give you the shits? All that fussin' round, all that whingein' about houses, and clothes, and food, and money, and God knows what.

STEVIE: And babies.

BRETT: [*laughing, to* GLENN] And salad bowls, eh mate? Fuckin' salad bowls.

GLENN: You don't know the half of it, all the shit you been puttin' on me about that bitch. Jesus, once you start livin' with one of 'em, it's like you're trapped. In her territory. Aw, fuck, mate, I been to hell and back. It's like they're puttin' a spell on you that sucks away everythin' that makes you a man.

STEVIE: Yeah, they do, don't they, it's your manhood what's at stake.

GLENN: Mate, the things they do when they're on home ground, it's just plain fuckin' disgustin'. Shavin' their legs in the shower, ruinin' your razor. Shit, and all that bleeding each month, all that funny stuff hangin' round the bathroom, what chance has a bloke got? Women are tainted, that's what they are, there's no other word for it.

STEVIE: Yeah, and it's time somebody cleaned 'em up.

BRETT: I don't know why we keep on lettin' 'em get away with it. I mean, a bloke's got enough shit to get through, just survivin'. All the stuff he's never goin' to do, never goin' to have. And about all those bitches do is remind a bloke what a piece of crap his life is. Fuck, why do we let 'em get away with it?

GLENN: I don't know, shit, why do we?

STEVIE: Yeah, we must be fuckin' mad.

BRETT: I mean, here we are, three brothers, best mates, been through everything together, and look at us, standin' here like stunned fuckin' mullets, not able to do nothin', not able to drive nowhere, no more grog, no nothin', and all because of them. Fuck 'em! Any man did that sort of thing to your life, you'd punish him, wouldn't you, you'd have the mongrel for breakfast. Only just 'cause they're chicks, we go on lettin' 'em get away with it. And I'll tell you, I'm not goin' to no more, I'm fucking not!

STEVIE: Yeah, why are we still standin' round puttin' up with it? Are we fuckin' mad or somethin'?

BRETT: Come on, the longer we stand round moanin' about it, the more it is they're winnin'. Let's just go somewhere and do somethin', like we're entitled to. If we haven't got a car, we'll take one, and we'll do anythin' we fuckin' like, no holds barred. Let's see 'em try to stop us!

GLENN: Yeah, I'm with you, that's for sure. [*He waves toward the house.*] Fuck you, ya bitch, I'll be thinkin' of ya! Only the things I'll be thinkin', you wouldn't want to know about!

STEVIE *waves towards the house.*

STEVIE: Yeah, you too, you stupid fat ugly bitch! I hope it comes out the wrong way and kills ya!

BRETT: Just let 'em get in our way, eh? One more fuckin' stupid bitch come interferin' in our lives, show up somewhere she shouldn't. She'll find out, you don't mess with the boys no more! Fuck 'em all!

BRETT, GLENN *and* STEVIE *go. Blackout.*

SCENE FOUR

Months later. The living room just before dawn. The room is in semi-darkness, with the curtains drawn. SANDRA *lies asleep on the cane lounge. From the outside comes the sound of a car approaching rapidly, slowing down, then the smash of a window, then the car moving away. A moment later there comes the sound of a baby crying, frantically.* SANDRA *does not stir. Moments later* JACKIE *enters, fastening a dressing-gown. She goes to the window.*

JACKIE: [*calling*] We haven't done anything! Leave us alone! You don't know what it's like for us.

> *She turns back from the window, realising the futility of her words. She addresses* SANDRA, *without paying much attention to her.*

They don't know what it's like for us. What do they think's going on in here?

> *She looks more closely at* SANDRA, *and is suddenly curious. Outside, the baby's crying quietens.*

Sandra?

> *She touches* SANDRA, *who does not stir.*

Sandra?

> MICHELLE *enters.*

MICHELLE: What's going on?

JACKIE: Don't know. Sandra won't wake up.

> MICHELLE *goes over to* SANDRA.

MICHELLE: Sandra?

> *She touches* SANDRA, *who does not stir. Then she bends down for a closer look.*

She's still breathing.

JACKIE: Yes, I can see that.

> MICHELLE *stands back from* SANDRA.

MICHELLE: I think her mind's going.

JACKIE: How's the baby?

MICHELLE: Alright. Bits of glass went everywhere, but the baby didn't get cut or anything, just scared. Who wouldn't be?

JACKIE: And Nola?

MICHELLE: Alright. [*She goes to the window and looks out.*] What do they want from us?

JACKIE: That's what I keep asking.

MICHELLE: I mean, it's not like we did anything, is it?

JACKIE: No. You'd think we were witches.

MICHELLE: Prowlin' round. Molestin' us in the street. Bricks through the window.

JACKIE: And they keep asking this one stupid question that's driving me up the wall. They keep saying, 'But those men had girlfriends'. As if what was done to that poor girl was just about sex.

MICHELLE: Eh?

JACKIE: They think, God, what sort of women must they be, what sort of lives must they lead, what sort of things must they have let those men do to them? As if we were having a nonstop orgy. As if we set the boys up.

MICHELLE: As if all the violence there is is our fault.

> SANDRA *stirs.* JACKIE *and* MICHELLE *watch.* SANDRA *half sits up bewildered.*

SANDRA: Is it morning yet?

MICHELLE: Yeah. But real early, you know?

SANDRA: Was having some sort of dream. Gee, I sleep heavy now, so heavy it's almost something else. And in this dream. Don't know when it was supposed to be, but Brett and Glenn and Stevie, they were only little, playin' with their toys, only somehow… they were big men as well. I couldn't understand it.

MICHELLE: Well, dreams are like that.

SANDRA: And then their toys turned into, must have been beer bottles, really big old ones, and they started smashin' them, over everything, over each other, over me, aw, it was terrifying, just smash, smash, smash, louder and louder.

MICHELLE: A window got broken, Sandra. You probably heard that.

SANDRA: A window?

MICHELLE: Yeah, some gutless wonder came burnin' by and lobbed a brick through a window. Into the room where Nola and the baby are.

SANDRA: Oh, no!

> SANDRA *tries to sit up, but has some difficulty.*

MICHELLE: It's alright, they're okay.

SANDRA: I want to go to them. To poor Nola and my little grandson. I want them to know I'm with 'em.

MICHELLE: Nola knows that. Why don't you stay where you are?

JACKIE: Yes, Sandra, maybe you should rest a bit longer.

> SANDRA *struggles up off the lounge with great difficulty, appearing weak and unsteady.*

SANDRA: No, I want to be with them. They might have taken Stevie away, but I'm part of him, and that little baby's part of him, and Nola's part of him too, we're all family. And if I have to use up all me strength bein' with 'em, well, that's just too bad. I mean, otherwise, what's it all for?

> SANDRA *takes a halting, wobbly step, then crashes to the floor.* MICHELLE *and* JACKIE *rush to her, alarmed. They try to help her up, but as she struggles back to her feet, she shrugs their attentions away.*

JACKIE: I think you'd better go back to that hospital, Sandra.

SANDRA: No, I'm not goin' to, I'm needed here. [*She takes a few steps, moving closer to the door.*] No, that rotten hospital, not going near that place again. Bein' gawked at by everyone. Bein' poked at by strangers in the waitin' room, and the doctors and nurses. All of 'em saying, 'You know who that is, you know who that is?' [*She takes a couple more steps.*] No, this is the only place I belong. Here with the spirit of me sons.

> SANDRA *leaves.*

JACKIE: She's missed all her treatment, you know. She's not getting any of the medication she's supposed to have.

MICHELLE: No.

JACKIE: Just doesn't seem to care about herself.

MICHELLE: No. Was when it finally came out that Glenn did it. Since then it's been like she's just, not botherin' anymore.

JACKIE: No. Can hardly even get her to eat anything.

MICHELLE: She held up so well, too, for so long. Tower of strength, she was. Still, I suppose there has to be a limit, and when Glenn gave in, well, so did she. [*Pause.*] Don't get me wrong. About Glenn. I mean nothing's changed for me.

JACKIE: Hasn't it?

MICHELLE: The police probably had to do all sorts of things to get that confession out of Glenn. I still believe in him, just as much as I believe in Brett and Stevie.

JACKIE: Huh, it's alright for you, isn't it? Saying that. Suddenly it's not so bad for you, you can take a step back from it all. Here's Glenn saying, 'Yeah, I did it, the others were just along for the ride'. And deep down, you can just accept that, can't you, and get on with living again.

MICHELLE: No, I wouldn't just wash my hands of Glenn like that.

JACKIE: I would if I was in your position.

MICHELLE: Yeah, I know you would.

JACKIE: Be better than what you've got now, wouldn't it? You could just write off the others, say it was Glenn and maybe Stevie who did it, and just go on believing in Brett.

MICHELLE: How could I, Jackie? Come on. Brett's brothers, they're part of what makes him tick. The three of 'em, they work the same way, it's like they got the same sort of machinery driving 'em. And if I abandoned the other two, Jesus, it'd be like turning me back on Brett as well. How could I do that?

Pause.

JACKIE: You know them really well, don't you?

MICHELLE: Yeah.

JACKIE: So you must know. What actually happened. You know, don't you? Absolutely.

Pause.

MICHELLE: Alright, I know.

JACKIE: And it's not that stuff you told me, is it? Stuff you said I should have faith in. They did it, didn't they?

Long pause. MICHELLE *paces around.*

Come on. You've come close to saying it already. Might as well get it over with.

Pause.

MICHELLE: [*suddenly angry*] Alright! They did it! They hacked that girl to pieces! They raped her and they killed her and they destroyed her!

JACKIE: And it was you and me they were doing it to. And Nola and probably Sandra as well.

MICHELLE *begins to sob.*

But I'm just saying something you've known all along.

MICHELLE: But who the hell are you taking it on yourself to straighten me out? Wanting to stick the truth down my throat, no matter how much it hurts. [*She composes herself and ceases sobbing.*] But then maybe you didn't have as much to lose as I did. So maybe it didn't matter what you thought. You were just having a bit of a game with Glenn, just sort of dabbling.

JACKIE: Did it look like a game to you? To me it seemed like we were trying to make some sort of a life together.

MICHELLE: Yeah, alright, I suppose you were, in your own way.

JACKIE : In my own way, right! So probably you could say I was feeling pain in my own way too, but let me tell you, it's just as real as yours.

MICHELLE: I'm not saying it isn't.

JACKIE: You know why I could never do like you, and believe against all the odds? Because way back, the day after it happened, Glenn virtually told me, and what's more he took pleasure in telling me.

MICHELLE: What?

JACKIE: Not in so many words. But he stood there in front of me while the police came running up the stairs. Glaring into my eyes. I'd already heard what had happened to that girl, and he knew I'd heard, and he said, 'I didn't know I could hate so much until you came along. I hated her because I hate you. All of you.'

MICHELLE: Jesus.

JACKIE: And I remember telling you straight afterwards, about how I'd just stood there and watched him being dragged out, and I knew you were thinking, 'What a low-down pathetic coward she is'.

MICHELLE: Yeah. Yeah, that's what I was thinking.

JACKIE: I should have told you then.

MICHELLE: I'm glad you didn't.

JACKIE: Then, yesterday, when I heard he'd confessed, given all those details of what he'd done, I knew exactly why. He wanted me to hear all about it, to know what he would have liked to have done to me. What he was really doing was bragging about his hate. His hate for any woman, but most of all his hate for me.

> JACKIE *begins crying.* MICHELLE *embraces her, trying to comfort.* JACKIE*'s crying diminishes.*

MICHELLE: But, that time when I got really heavy and said you couldn't stay unless you came out and said Glenn and the rest were innocent. You really had me believing. You meant it.

JACKIE: I wanted to. God knows I tried hard enough. I'd invested so much, don't you see?

MICHELLE: Yes, I suppose I do.

JACKIE: I'd put every last bit of me into that relationship, into that life we had going. Concentrating, every single moment of the day, wanting to make it work. Perhaps I was trying too hard, I forgot to look at what I was really doing.

MICHELLE: Perhaps we all did that.

NOLA *enters, carrying a baby wrapped in a bundle.*

NOLA: Something's wrong with Sandra. She's fallen over.

MICHELLE: Oh no.

MICHELLE *pulls back from* JACKIE, *and leaves hurriedly.* JACKIE *sits down and composes herself more.* NOLA *goes to the window and looks out. She rocks the baby gently.*

JACKIE: They're long gone.

NOLA: Yeah. I just felt like looking out. [*Pause.*] Huh, what is there you'd want to look at out there? [*She turns away from the window.*] That's the worst thing. What this little bloke's goin' to see. I mean, I can't stop all that stuff that goes on. [*She paces up and down, rocking the baby gently.*] You know, what's the point of trying to lie about it anymore? That's just what it's like. And that's just what this little bloke's goin' to be like, unless some miracle happens. I can't just hide him in a cupboard, can I? Sooner or later he's going to go out there into the same world Stevie and Brett and Glenn lived in, and why should he be any different from them? It'd take a lot more than I got to do anything about it. [*Pause.*] I mean Stevie, he might not have fitted into things real well, but he wasn't a freak, neither. None of them were. They were just, like, part of somethin'.

JACKIE: Sounds like you got it all worked out.

NOLA: No. Not by a long shot. But I'll tell you, I've had plenty of time to think about it, these last few months. Sittin' there in that room starin' at me tummy while it all went on outside. Thinkin' about that poor little kid in there, watchin' the ripples where he was jumpin' up and down, wonderin' what was goin' to happen to him. [*Pause.*] Yeah, hah, you know the first thing I said to meself after the birth? I said, thank God it's not a girl. 'Cause I'd been thinkin', you know, about what happened to that girl that night. Thinkin' about all sorts of things blokes might do to my girl if she was pretty, and all the things she'd have to cop if she wasn't. [*Pause.*] I mean, I s'pose you can try getting by just being on your own and that, but jeez, they make it tough for you. They make you feel like you're missin' out on so much if you can't go along with it all, can't be the sort of girl who has blokes after her all the time. All that sort of playing games and putting it on you're supposed to do. [*Pause.*] Yeah, they make it so tantalising. For the blokes as well, I suppose. Even little Stevie, you know, even him, he might seem like a little worm when he's on his own, but when he's with the others, being part of all that, acting the way they do, yeah, it's like suddenly he's a foot taller. It's that thing you see all the time, on street corners and outside pubs, and when you see them hanging out of their cars. That thing that holds them together and makes them act the same as each other, whatever they're like inside. But this extra thing they have together, it's full of nothing but evil. [*Pause.*] But this evil, all this violence and hatred, they think they're using it. But it's using them! [*Pause.*] And it'll use this little bloke, too. And what can I do to stop it?

JACKIE: Don't ask me. I tried hard enough, I couldn't do anything.

NOLA: But there must be something you can do, mustn't there? I mean, when he's this young, this little, he doesn't know anything. So maybe I could... I don't know. At least stop some of those things getting to him. Make him see what crap it all is, all that stuff he's supposed to believe in. [*Pause.*] I know what you're thinking. What can a hopeless dag like her do?

JACKIE: No, I wasn't thinking that. I was thinking, perhaps we could try and do it together.

NOLA: You were?

JACKIE: We must be able to give him something from what we've learned out of all this. Show him he doesn't really have to hate us, whatever they tell him.

NOLA *continues pacing back and forth, rocking the baby.* SANDRA *and* MICHELLE *enter.* SANDRA *is staggering, lurching, but resisting* MICHELLE*'s efforts to help.*

SANDRA: No, love, it's alright, I'm not the one who needs any help.

MICHELLE: Come on, Sandra. Lie down again. At least do that.

SANDRA: Yeah, alright, I will put me feet up, I wouldn't mind that. But don't go talking about doctors. There's no-one can help now except God, and I reckon if he was goin' to do anythin' he would have done it by now. To all of us.

SANDRA *lies down on the couch. The others watch as she settles back.*

JACKIE: Anything we can get you?

SANDRA: No, love, my needs are small. All I ask is a bit of loving from my family, and I've never been short of that.

JACKIE: Well, you just have to ask. We're here to look after you.

SANDRA: Tell you what I would like. A hold of that baby.

NOLA: Yeah, for sure.

NOLA *hands the baby to* SANDRA, *who holds it close to her.*

SANDRA: Hey, little fella. You look just like your dad, you know that, when he was a tiny little thing. He was just like you. So were his brothers. Ah, it's amazing, you could be any one of them. Oh, just look at you.

NOLA: [*to* JACKIE *and* MICHELLE] He doesn't. He looks like me. He doesn't look like his father at all.

JACKIE: [*to* NOLA] You're right. The only person he looks like is his mother.

SANDRA *holds the baby away from her to look at it. She fumbles the baby and the others move in anxiously, fearing she'll drop it.*

MICHELLE: You right there? You want us to take him back for a bit?

SANDRA: No, don't worry, I'll keep a firm grip on him. I might be all broken down, but one thing that's still goin' strong is me motherin' instincts. [*She fondles the baby.*] Yes, yes, I won't let you go, don't you worry, you're safe and sound with me. Ah, yes, my little son, ah, my little son.

JACKIE: Well, it's your grandson, Sandra.

MICHELLE *nudges* JACKIE *to keep quiet.*

MICHELLE: Let her believe what she likes. Won't make any difference now.

SANDRA: Ah, all the joys you and your two little brothers are going to bring me. All the rewards. Yes, looking at you, how could a mum think there was anything bad in the whole wide world?

SANDRA *hums gently as she rocks the baby, then sinks further back onto the lounge.* NOLA *moves in and takes the baby from her, and* SANDRA *does not resist.* NOLA *moves away towards the door, rocking the baby gently. The others stand watching.*

THE END